CONTENTS

Abbreviations and acronymns   2

1   Musicians in Ukraine   2
2   Battle of Bakhmut   10
3   Mutiny of June 2023   27
4   Critical Perception of the Wagner Group   48
5   Conclusions   52

Endnotes   54
About the Authors   64

Helion & Company Limited
Unit 8 Amherst Business Centre
Budbrooke Road
Warwick
CV34 5WE
England
Tel. 01926 499 619
Email: info@helion.co.uk
Website: www.helion.co.uk
Twitter: @helionbooks
https://helionbooks.wordpress.com/

Text © János Besenyö, András István Türke, and Endre Szénási, with Tom Cooper 2025
Colour profiles: Giorgio Albertini, David Bocquelet, Tom Cooper
Maps: Tom Cooper & Anderson Subtil

Cover image: A Wagner mercenary posing in front of a ruined building in Bakhmut, Ukraine, in late May 2023. (via Dean O'Brien)

Designed and typeset by Mach 3 Solutions (www.mach3solutions.co.uk)
Cover design Paul Hewitt, Battlefield Design (www.battlefield-design.co.uk)

Every reasonable effort has been made to trace copyright holders and to obtain their permission for the use of copyright material. The author and publisher apologise for any errors or omissions in this work, and would be grateful if notified of any corrections that should be incorporated in future reprints or editions of this book.

ISBN: 978-1-804516-10-2

British Library Cataloguing-in-Publication Data
A catalogue record for this book is available from the British Library

All rights reserved. No part of this publication may be reproduced, stored in a retrieval system, or transmitted, in any form, or by any means, electronic, mechanical, photocopying, recording or otherwise, without the express written consent of Helion & Company Limited.

We always welcome receiving book proposals from prospective authors.

Note: In order to simplify the use of this book, all names, locations and geographic designations are as provided in *The Times World Atlas*, or other traditionally accepted major sources of reference, as of the time of described events.

ABBREVIATIONS AND ACRONYMNS

BTG	Battalion Tactical Group
CAA	Combined Arms Army (Russian)
GRU	*Glavnoje Razvedyvatel'noje Upravlenije* (Main Intelligence Directorate) (of Russia)
MOD	Ministry of Defence (Russia or Ukraine)
PMC	Private Military Company/Private Military Contractor
UAV	unmanned aerial vehicle
USSR	Union of Soviet Socialist Republics (also, Soviet Union)
VDV	*Vozdushno-desantnye voyska* (Airborne Forces) (Russia)
VKS	Russian Aerospace Force
VSRF	Armed Forces of the Russian Federation
ZSU	Ukrainian Armed Forces

1
MUSICIANS IN UKRAINE

The Russian political decision to seize Crimea[1] was based on information that the Russian Black Sea Fleet would, sooner rather than later, be ousted from Sevastopol in order to be replaced by NATO warships and military presence.[2] Such ideas and plans were widely supported by Ukrainian politicians running for the presidency, as electoral promises, and part of their political programme. Should a 'second Maidan' have occurred in Sevastopol, Moscow would have had two basic (classic) choices. One possibility was to withdraw the Black Sea Fleet: no matter under what circumstances the still existing Fleet Agreement would be breached by the parties.[3] Such a move would have demonstrated Russia's weakness and would not reflect the image that Vladimir Vladimirovich Putin wanted for Russia. Another option for Moscow was to defend the presence of the Black Sea Fleet by military force: that would result in a bloodbath, especially taking into consideration that masses of armed Ukrainian civilians would have been part of the conflict. Neither scenario was acceptable for Moscow. Therefore, Russia did not wait for a 'second Maidan' to take place but took the initiative. However, this initiative was quite unorthodox and unusual due to ambiguity and deniability provided by the operational engagement of the Wagner Group.

Wagner's Role Prior to February 2022

The Wagner Group private military company (PMC) was first deployed in Crimea in 2014,[4] when officially unidentified 'little green men' appeared and occupied Crimea facing virtually no resistance at all.[5] These men wore no national insignia, such as Russian flags, no badges, no unit numbers, no nametags, and always had covered faces when in public. The category of 'officially unidentified' is important to understand. On one hand it allowed the Russian leadership to officially deny a Russian military presence in Crimea, on the other hand use of Russian uniforms and equipment was done on purpose: Ukrainian soldiers, mostly ethnic Russians in Crimea had to know that they were facing mostly very well-trained Wagner fighters and Russian Special Operations Forces and clearly not some poorly-trained militias.

The Wagner Group, and especially Prigozhin, gained a higher visibility once the Russian-Ukrainian war entered a new stage from 24 February 2022. While the international community tended to call the events of February 2022 the 'start of the Russian-Ukrainian war', this was denied by official Russian policy, suggesting that war had been ongoing since 2014 due to the Ukrainian side 'relentlessly shelling the civilian population and infrastructure of Donbass'. Therefore, according to the official policy of the Kremlin, the war between Russia and Ukraine did not start in 2022. On the other hand, the Russian leadership, including Putin, claimed, that a Ukrainian attack to 'liberate' Donbass was imminent, and Russia would not make the same strategic mistake as she did in 1941 when the Union of Soviet Socialist Republics (USSR; colloquially 'Soviet Union') waited for a German attack to happen first. According to the official Russian position concerning the issue, following that historic example would have led to a serious disadvantage and unnecessary casualties on the side of the local Russian population.

What followed during the Russian all-out invasion of Ukraine, beginning in late February and extending through March 2022, was a series of unexpected developments. Anticipating a swift collapse of Ukraine's armed forces and expecting the population to welcome Russian troops as liberators, Vladimir Putin and his advisors planned an operation that was effectively a coup. This involved a combination of special forces and heliborne assaults, followed by a rapid advance of ground forces. However, the Ukrainians mounted fierce resistance, and the initial plan, known as 'Plan A,' fell apart within the first 24 hours. Undeterred but emboldened by the Russian military's early advances in southern Ukraine, Putin, along with his Minister of Defence, Sergey Shoygu, and the Chief of the General Staff, Valery Gerasimov, pivoted to 'Plan B.' This new strategy aimed to secure or isolate Kyiv through simultaneous assaults by mechanised forces from multiple directions. However, this plan also collapsed for a variety of reasons, including Putin's persistent micromanagement and the institutionalized corruption and incompetence within the Russian Armed Forces (VSRF). Even Russia's ostensibly elite units were poorly prepared for the complex operations they were tasked with executing. Repeated attempts to push mechanised columns into Kyiv from the northwest and west resulted in devastating losses. Efforts to seize

Chernihiv and advance on Kyiv from the north-east were thwarted by internal disorganization and significant casualties among the Combined Arms Army (CAA) units involved. Meanwhile, two additional and ostensibly powerful CAAs attempting to reach the Ukrainian capital from the east failed to capture Sumy and suffered crippling losses due to Ukrainian ambushes and attacks on their overstretched supply lines.[6] Ultimately, Russian forces were forced to abandon their plans not only for Kyiv but also for Chernihiv, Sumy, and Kharkiv, refocusing their attention on eastern Ukraine. Although the VSRF withdrew all remaining forces from northern and north-eastern Ukraine as ordered, subsequent offensives on Sloviansk, Sievierodonetsk, and Lysychansk devolved into grueling battles of attrition that even Russia's forces could not sustain. Any breakthroughs achieved by Russian troops were limited in scope and came at an enormous cost in lives and equipment. By July 2022, Russian forces finally secured Lyman, Sievierodonetsk, and Lysychansk, but by this point, the peacetime army that had initiated the invasion was shattered and incapable of continuing large-scale offensive operations.

Amid these setbacks, the Wagner Group re-emerged as a significant player. Early in the invasion, this PMC was neither prominent nor particularly missed by the Ukrainians or their Western supporters. However, over the following months, Russian media increasingly portrayed Wagner as the most reliable and capable force fighting for Russia's interests in Ukraine.

In turn, because the war activities that Russia officially called their 'Special Military Operation' were considered to be a success by Moscow, and the Wagner Group played a prominent role, the rise of Prigozhin to high level politics appeared to be inevitable. Prigozhin had already claimed that he intended to take part in the

Yevgeny Prigozhin, boss of the Wagner Group. In his public appearances during 2022, he was still insistent that his PMC was a 'fully independent force', not reporting to the VSRF or the Ministry of Defence in Moscow. (Wagner Group, via Grey Zone)

2024 presidential elections in Russia.[7] If Putin wanted to annihilate Prigozhin's chances to become a president, he could have further cut the financing of this PMC until a deal was achieved, or changed the law according to which Prigozhin, a formerly convicted prisoner in Russia, was unfit to participate in presidential elections. Putin could also have decided to 'make Prigozhin disappear'.

Detachments of the Wagner Group were first deployed to Donbas in 2014–2015, where its primary task was that of bringing the local separatist militias under Putin's control. (Grey Zone)

Special Military Operation and Framework for Wagner Deployment

The deployment of Wagner PMC to Ukraine was always done with the direct support of the Russian government and its armed forces. Thus, in order to understand Wagner's role in the war we need to come up with an analysis of the war itself, focusing on issues making it easier to understand the challenges Wagner PMC had to face.

Even though the Kremlin officially calls the war in Ukraine a 'Special Military Operation', most Western and Eastern politicians, experts, and journalists do not refer to it that way and instead refer to it as a 'war', 'full scale war', 'invasion' or similar. Even enthusiastically pro-Russian analysts tend to call it a 'war', rather than a 'Special Military Operation'. Several pro-Russian military reporters initially tended to call it a 'Special Military Operation' at the beginning of major Russian operations from 24 February 2022, but later on when its scale became obvious, they tended to call it 'war'.

This sub-chapter we will not get into the details of Moscow's decision to launch their 'Special Military Operation' on 24 February 2022, such as Russian policies opposing NATO's Eastern expansion etc, because that topic goes beyond the scope of examining the Wagner Group's role in Ukraine. However, we might clarify, that based on the Kremlin's official position, the 'war' in Ukraine (this is precisely the term the Kremlin uses), did not start in 2022, when the 'Special Military Operation' started, but in 2014, following the removal of the former Ukrainian president Viktor Janukovich.

Based on Putin's declaration, the aim of the 'Special Military Operation' was a 'demilitarisation and de-Nazification' of the whole of Ukraine. This sub-chapter will make use of the Russian terminology, quoted in inverted commas, to help enable a precise understanding of that terminology, while also making it possible to maintain a distance from that terminology for those who disagree with the substance of it. Putin could have framed the term 'de-Nazification'[8] differently, perhaps as 'combating far-right elements' or 'removing the far-right from power.' However, this would not have made the Russian terminology more politically palatable – especially in Western contexts, where it caused confusion and led some to misleadingly adopt Kremlin rhetoric. Moreover, the term 'de-Nazification' is widely interpreted as targeting all levels of Ukrainian society where such elements are perceived, whereas 'removing the far-right from power' implies a narrower focus on eliminating certain individuals from key positions rather than addressing society as a whole. Such misinterpretations hinder efforts to accurately present the realities of the war in Ukraine.

At the beginning of the 'Special Military Operation' Moscow also stressed, that its aims did not include the overthrowing of the Ukrainian leadership. It was strange indeed, but it reflected that Moscow intended to force a peace agreement upon Ukraine purely based on the fact that a Russian military intervention was underway. The Kremlin later claimed that they were close to a peace agreement in Istanbul, but the Ukrainian leadership decided not to sign such an agreement, and not to get into compromises concerning sovereignty and territorial integrity of the country.

What does the 'Special Military Operation' mean? The Russian arguments will be presented here, since the Wagner Group was Russian, in order to render more understandable what Wagner PMC did on the battlefields of Ukraine.

'Demilitarisation' meant the destruction of Ukrainian military capabilities to an extent necessary to force (dictate) a peace agreement on Kyiv. At the beginning of the 'Special Military Operation' Moscow tacitly believed, that it would be enough to fire upon Ukrainian National Guard 'far-right formations' in order to pacify the Ukrainian Armed Forces, which in turn would then not shoot at Russian forces entering Ukraine. Thus, removing the armed, hardliner nationalist 'and far-right' elements by itself could be enough to change the entire political course of Ukraine. Moscow proved to be very wrong in its assessment for not the first time, and not the last time since the 'Special Military Operation' started. The Ukrainian Armed Forces not only fired upon Russian forces entering Ukraine, but resisted them with all their capabilities.

There are two possible interpretations of what happened. According to the most common interpretation, Moscow made an unsubstantiated, unprofessional and naïve political decision that proved to be fatally wrong. Another interpretation might suggest that Moscow provided a chance to Kyiv to save an enormous number of human lives during the armed conflict, which the Ukrainian leadership rejected. Since it was not the only case during the Ukraine war when Kyiv had a chance to settle the conflict, but at the end chances were wasted, such an interpretation might deserve attention. The Minsk Agreements were a good example of that. It is far from the authors' intention to get into a 'blame-game' and solely criticise one or another party when the chances of a peace settlement were missed. It is also the belief that compromises with Moscow can, could, and should always be debated, but the bottom line is to what extent the war could go on serving genuine Ukrainian interests and where the boundaries lie, when it goes beyond Ukraine's genuine interests, leading to unnecessary sacrifices when the price would ultimately, and mostly, be paid by the Ukrainian people. Several unsuccessful and very bloody Ukrainian counteroffensives that failed to gain any significant territory, have been a good example of that.[9] To put it simply, but clearly and understandably: it was in only one case that Ukraine had the qualitative and the quantitative superiority necessary for a successful counteroffensive. General Ben Hodges, former Commander of US Forces in Europe emphasised the necessity of air superiority for successful offensive operations, without which no American, British or German soldiers would ever have been ordered to advance.[10] Valery Zaluhzny, the Commander-in-Chief of the Ukrainian Armed Forces from 2019 until 2023, also confirmed that.[11] He could not, and he would not, go as far as to publicly admit that the failure of the Ukrainian counteroffensives was foreseeable.[12] His analysis was designed for international audiences in order to cool expectations related to the Ukrainian counteroffensive, when Western disappointment was 'in the air', widely admitted and seen as a bad omen for the NATO summit in July 2023.

For those who might still be sceptical concerning Ukraine's chances to win a resource war against Russia, a clear reminder might be the number of soldiers recruited to the opposing militaries. While Ukraine had a population of 30 million people remaining in the country, and Russia had a population of 140 million people, the following numbers might make sense for an analysis. Ukraine has never declared 'full mobilisation': between the late February 2022 and early 2024, it has recruited all males between the age of 27 and 59, including those with no military background. As of September 2022, this allowed the Ukrainian Armed Forces (ZSU) to field nearly twice as many troops as the Russian Armed Forces (VSRF) had deployed in the country. However, significant mismanagement, corruption, and incompetence within the Ukrainian General Staff, combined with Western hesitation and a tendency to appease Putin through half-hearted decisions and delays in delivering heavy weaponry to Kyiv, created a challenging situation. As a result, the ZSU managed to launch only one successful large-scale offensive: the September 2022 operation, which recaptured eastern Kharkiv and Lyman and nearly pushed the VSRF back into western Luhansk province.

'Russians in need of being saved': members of the Luhansk People's Republic 'armed forces', with one of their MT-LB armoured personnel carriers. (Russian social media)

In contrast, Russia only initiated its mobilization in late September 2022. Even then, the process was slow due to the VSRF's inability to handle more than 25,000 to 30,000 newly mobilized troops at a time. Challenges included providing these soldiers with uniforms and weapons, offering even minimal refresher training, and organising them into cohesive units before deploying them to the battlefield. Moreover, it was limited to between 1.0–1.1 percent of the available population, that included only those who had a military background, and where certain professionals were excluded (such as computer scientists and those working for the defence industry). The amount of human reserves by itself might be enough to tell the enormous difference between Ukraine and Russia.[13]

De jure, Putin's 'de-Nazification' referred, in politically correct terms, to the 'neutralization' of neo-Nazi elements, particularly those organised into armed formations. *De facto*, however, it signified the eradication of any form of Ukrainian resistance to Putin's regime.[14] International political leaders and analysts were well aware of the issue, however, they tend to be rather silent about this, or flatly deny it,[15] since they felt that it was a phenomenon useful against Russia. Interestingly, some authors had been very enthusiastic to prove that Putin's arguments concerning 'de-Nazification' were entirely wrong, false, or even absurd when Russia invaded Ukraine on 24 February 2022, and for a few months after the beginning of the Russian invasion.[16] However, the Ukraine war has demonstrated a number of 'unfortunate events' and this enthusiasm to deny the very existence of problems with 'far-right elements' in Ukraine 'lost much of its pace', since it was realised that the issue was becoming increasingly difficult to be easily 'swept under the carpet'.

'De-Nazification' was a very interesting issue. Because it was intended to be conducted across all of Ukraine, it raised questions by itself, especially concerning the end state of the Ukraine war. The key question was whether the whole of Ukraine had to be occupied by Russia, or not, in order to achieve this goal? The Kremlin never provided any reasonable answers but some analysts did. According to the opinion of top Russian geo-political- and military analysts, 'de-Nazification' was only possible based on the will of the entirety, or at least an overwhelming percentage, of Ukrainian society. This would require a change of the constitution, and also the rest of the legal environment, as well as the education system. However, it could not be achieved based on a 'peace agreement' when none of the parties have the political will to fulfil it, as could be witnessed in case of the Minsk Agreements.

A 'strange war' is truly a synonym for the 'Special Military Operation' on the Russian side, with no exaggeration. 'Strange war' is the authors' term, unlike 'demilitarisation' and 'de-Nazification', that are terms of the Kremlin. 'Strange war' has been placed in inverted commas since its substance is quite debatable, even though there are many signs that prove that war in Ukraine is full of controversy and contradictions. However, the authors believe that it is worth analysing, since such an analysis highlights some key aspects of the war that could change in the future and that could significantly affect the nature and the outcome of the armed conflict in Ukraine.

Abstaining from overthrowing the Kyiv-regime ('regime change') is a ridiculous idea on the Kremlin's side, even though it was widely propagated from the beginning. How could it ever been taken seriously that that Moscow 'only' wanted to 'de-Nazify' Ukraine, as a whole, while not overthrowing its leadership, supporting whatever happens in their country, including the far-right movement, armed, and actively employed for the purposes of the Ukrainian state? Such declarations could not be taken seriously at all, because it was always obvious that an elected Ukrainian leadership would never go as far as to 'de-Nazify' Ukraine, no matter what 'peace agreement' or 'peace dictate' it may have signed. Unsurprisingly, at the time of this analysis there was no 'peace agreement' in sight at all.

It is indeed a 'strange war' when the Ukrainian 'centres of decision making', such as Parliament (Rada), the presidential residence, the Ministry of Defence (MOD) and other Ukrainian ministries, were not targeted by Russian airstrikes[17] (buildings of security services, field command centres etc. as strictly military targets are indeed targeted by Russia[18]) – not even when Moscow was drawing red lines and promised to attack the decision makers in Kyiv in the event of Ukrainian attacks on the territory of the Russian Federation with long-range weapons.[19] Attacking such critical infrastructure like nuclear power plants made it even worse.[20] Unkept promises and 'flexible red lines' were thus additional features of Moscow's 'strange war' and to such an extent that key western leaders – like US President Joe Biden, NATO Secretary General Jens Stoltenberg, former Prime Minister of the United Kingdom Boris Johnson, Chancellor of Germany Olaf Scholz, and others – were able to frequently visit Zelensky in Kyiv. It is exactly the same that happened during the 2008 Georgian war,[21] when Moscow abstained from bombing similar targets, including the International Airport in Tbilisi.

It is a 'strange war', when top level politicians attempt to talk seriously about an invitation and an acceptance of Ukraine – at war with Russia – to NATO. [22] Former NATO Secretary General Rasmussen and Zelensky are just two of them.

Russia is not similar to Serbia, when in conflict with NATO, leaving open the possibility of its annihilation, as an adversary of the Alliance. Russia is a *nuclear* superpower (otherwise not), which has theoretical capabilities to conduct nuclear strikes equivalent to that of the United States of America. These two nuclear superpowers have the capabilities to terminate human life on Earth: all other nuclear powers are far behind the two leaders in this regard. An early invitation and an acceptance of Ukraine to NATO – existing in a *de facto* state of war – could result in two major scenarios:

- Scenario No.1 being a direct war between Russia and NATO, that would be highly likely to lead to a nuclear war between the Alliance and Russia, exactly as many leaders and experts believe,[23] ultimately exterminating human life on Earth. This was an entirely mad scenario, no doubt of that.
- Scenario No.2 was making Ukraine a member of NATO, then not undertaking any serious actions, including abstention from any serious military action aimed at regaining lost Ukrainian territories. In such a scenario, Article V would be excluded, thus making the Ukrainian membership in the alliance pointless. Many countries would analyse the situation and concluded that security guarantees by NATO, including Article V, were entirely dependent on the aggressor. Should the aggressor be a potent nuclear power, Article V would be meaningless.

Both scenarios could be disastrous for NATO and could be even more disastrous regarding the interests of the survival of humanity. It needs to be added to such an analysis that Putin's Russia was highly unlikely to completely withdraw from Ukraine, providing the 'soft landing' of Ukraine's NATO accession. Integrating Ukraine into NATO step-by-step or divided into parts similarly made no sense, even though it was suggested by former NATO secretary Rasmussen. Luckily, sober minds appear to have won amongst the top decision makers of the Alliance: Ukraine did not get an invitation to NATO at the Vilnius Summit, neither did it get any details concerning a timeline for accession. NATO Secretary General Jens Stoltenberg made it clear once again that without a Ukrainian military victory against Russia the question of Ukraine's accession to NATO would not arise.[24] US President Joe Biden also excluded the accession of Ukraine to NATO prior to a resolution of the Ukraine war.[25]

It is a 'strange war', when neither Russia, nor Ukraine have officially declared a state of war.[26] Russia did not declare a war against Georgia in 2008, however, the war was resolved in a few days, thus making the declaration of war irrelevant. Russia did declare a state of war following the blowing up of the Kerch bridge (Ukraine has recently acknowledged responsibility for that event, which was called 'state terrorism' by Moscow), the regions bordering Ukraine, and the regions included in the updated Russian Constitution as parts of the Russian Federation, however, there was no declaration of war between Russia as a whole and Ukraine as a whole, and this is unlikely to ever occur. The possibility of a Russian declaration of state of war draws no attention in Russian mainstream media.

It is a 'strange war', when Russia mostly abstains from bombing the bridges[27] and ports[28] that Ukraine uses to supply their troops on the Eastern front, including the delivery of Western military technology and fuel. With the exception of the Russian military withdrawal from Kherson on the right bank of the Dnieper, where the Russians blew up two bridges to prevent Ukrainian troops from following them,[29] almost all the news in the international media reported has Ukrainian bombardment of bridges on the Dnipro River[30] rather than any Russian attempts to do so. Even the Ukrainian counteroffensive did not persuade Russia's top political decision makers to bombard bridges on the Dnipro. The authors' interpretation of the strange Russian policy is that they want the Ukrainian Armed Forces to attack Russian defensive lines on the eastern front and suffer heavy casualties rather than allowing them to survive beyond the right bank of the Dnipro.

Prior to the Russian withdrawal from the 'grain deal,[31] Moscow abstained from bombing Ukrainian port infrastructure. A major Russian policy goal was to end weapon deliveries to Ukraine by ships on their way back to Ukrainian ports, where the grain deal was used as cover, and which was a violation of the grain deal. The explosion at a Turkish port on 7 August 2023 might well have been evidence of denied shipments,[32] even though the initial evaluation officially suggested that the cause of the powerful explosion destroying Turkish grain silos was 'wheat dust compression'.[33] What made the incident suspicious was the timing and the huge power of the explosion, and that similar events did not occur prior to the Russian withdrawal from the grain deal. It was politically correct to accuse Moscow of purposefully creating a global food shortage by withdrawing from the grain deal, and thus allowing the sale of grain (including both Russian grain, and grain stolen from occupied parts of Ukraine) for higher prices. This not only increased food prices but also caused shortages in Asia and Africa, undermining the Russian influence there. Following the Russian withdrawal from the deal, it became a Russian priority to destroy Ukrainian port infrastructure to make the revival of the grain deal impossible. Still, Russia largely abstained from attacking vessels from various countries as these were underway to and from Ukrainian ports.[34] It unclear to what extent Russia succeeded in the destruction of Ukrainian port infrastructure. Even though Moscow claims that the door to the revival of the grain deal remains open, the authors consider it unlikely to occur in the short run.

It is a 'strange war' when Germany's Rheinmetall constructed an arms factory in Subcarpathia, in Ukraine, tasked to service, repair and produce armoured military vehicles, including tanks and armoured personnel carriers. At least the reasoning was unusual: Ukraine would have to supply itself on its own, and not be solely dependent on Western military aid. Was anybody seriously convinced that Russia would not be aware of the precise coordinates of the German-built 'tank-factory'? Would anybody seriously think that Russia would not destroy such a factory, as a strategically important target? Would anybody seriously think that Ukraine would in the foreseeable future stand up successfully against the Russian war machine without immense Western political, financial, and military support? This decision was even more strange considering Germany refused to construct a factory to maintain and repair German-made Leopard tanks in Poland,[35] a much safer location.

It is a 'strange war', when Ukrainian far-right elements, declared as such by Moscow, are accused by Moscow of all sorts of war crimes (including murder, torture, and rape of civilians and prisoners of war) on a regular basis, are captured, investigated, promises were made by the Kremlin to bring them to justice, and then they were quietly exchanged as prisoners of war.[36] It remains a 'strange war' even when Turkey violates the agreement between Ankara, Moscow and Kyiv, by handing over former Ukrainian prisoners of war, described by Moscow as the leaders of the Azov regiment, to Kyiv.[37] Turkey's move to do so provoked outrage in Russian society, thus the entire system of capturing alive fighters viewed as neo-Nazis was brought into question. We know what the Geneva Convention is about and that such Russian conclusions in the pages of *Pravda* are an open call to violate the Geneva Convention. However, there were arguments supporting the Russian notion that terrorists and neo-Nazi leaders should get no mercy, must be executed on the spot when captured, being similarly treated as the worst terrorists.[38]

It is a 'strange war', when Ukrainian critical energy infrastructure, such as power plants, high voltage network, transformation stations, was virtually not targeted at all by Russian forces prior to the first successful bombing of the Kerch bridge connecting Russia with Crimea. There have been two successful attacks on the Kerch bridge, in October 2022 and in July 2023; Kyiv accepted responsibility for carrying out both.[39] The first successful attack on the Kerch bridge was followed by Russian retaliation targeting Ukrainian critical energy infrastructure, mostly connected to electricity generation and distribution.[40]

It is a 'strange war', when Russia announced the mobilisation of 300,000 personnel in the autumn of 2022, having a military background, and that the Kremlin has ever since insisted that there was 'no necessity' for a new mobilisation, although continuously mobilising additional reservists and volunteers at a rate of at least 30,000 a month. Will there ever be a rotation for these troops? Will any of them ever return home alive and uninjured? Will Russia endlessly continue this war without the necessary military force to achieve a decisive victory, limiting its mobilised pool of human resources to less than 1.1%?

It is a 'strange war' when Ukrainian drones attack the Kremlin with the aim of assassinating Putin,[41] and Russia's military response just fades away in the fog of war.

There are even more arguments to support the idea, that the Russian 'Special Military Operation' is the synonym of a 'strange war'. For that reason, anyone might consider calling what happens Ukraine a war, a full scale war, or a 'strange war', maybe a 'Special Military Operation', as they like.

What was Wagner Fighting for in Ukraine?

As in the case of all PMCs around the world – and, indeed, the mass of volunteers serving in the armed forces of the Russian Federation – Wagner's soldiers in Ukraine were fighting for money. Those who were recruited from prisons, were also fighting to be pardoned. It has never been sufficiently explained whether those having a criminal background were eligible for any sort of pardon that may allow them to have a clean record for the rest of their career. However, in the case of Ukraine this was not all. Ukraine was once part of tsarist Russia, and later part of the USSR, and became the territory with the largest ethnic Russian minority outside the country's borders. Although Kyiv has not released up-to-date demographic studies, millions of people in Ukraine still identify as Russian, and at least 50% of the population continues to use Russian as their everyday language. While a significant portion of the Russian minority has likely left Ukraine, many have chosen to remain. For such historic reasons the average Russian was not indifferent to what happened in Ukraine, even the soldiers serving in the Wagner Group. Noting the difference between Ukraine and other locations of armed conflicts where Wagner is present would make sense, since Wagner is (or has been) present in several countries in Africa and Latin America where their soldiers could be politically and historically indifferent to the conflict. On the other hand, it could be argued that the USSR had historic influence in Africa, Latin America and even Asia, so each country where Wagner was physically present deserves a case-by-case analysis of the past to determine some of the motivations of Wagner in the background, and also some of the good or bad memories of the Soviet presence, that could facilitate or be a burden on Wagner's operations.

Returning to Ukraine, there is a legal interpretation of what the Russian intervention means, mostly unquoted by Westerners, but it does not mean that such an interpretation is irrelevant to those who have fought for Wagner in Ukraine. The following arguments are not intended to support the Russian political arguments, nor to justify or deny the official opinions of opposing parties. The sole purpose of the following analysis is to explain the Russian position according to which the pro-Russian civilian population of historically Russian territories deserves special protection by the Russian Federation. This issue is far more complex than it appears at first glance, and was certainly relevant to those serving with Wagner PMC.

Whether Crimea belongs to Ukraine or Russia mainly depends on the legal interpretation of self-determination in International Law, which incorporates and acknowledges the institution of self-determination. However, an in-depth analysis, touching upon key issues of self-determination, is often missing. First of all, it needs to be acknowledged that according to the mainstream interpretation of International Law – which also means the interpretation by the majority of countries in the world – Crimea belongs to Ukraine. However, this is not the only interpretation that exists and highlights the national interests of Russia. There are also countries that have political reasons to vote on the side of Russia in the UN, or to abstain from voting.

International Law is a creation of the great powers, who all have their internal issues relating to minorities and their ambitions to push through some sort of self-determination. In Russia, there is, for example, Chechnya, that could in theory be eager to become an independent nation state. It is not by accident that the authors have selected Chechnya, that is part of Russia, as an example, and not another applicant elsewhere in the world. Chechnya is a perfect example of double standards, when a nation state allows, or even supports, self-determination in the case of one region, and decisively rejects it in case of another region. It should be kept in mind that there are plenty of regions around the world, that are eager to push through efforts to gain state sovereignty, such as Catalonia, Scotland, Taiwan, or even Texas – should the mainstream interpretation of International Law and the majority nation's interference not disturb their efforts. In the case of Catalonia, the majority nation is Spain, in case of Scotland it is the United Kingdom, in case of Taiwan it is China, in case of Texas it is the United States of America.

Chechnya has a different religion to most of Russia, that is Muslim, as opposed to Russian Eastern Orthodox Christianity. Chechnya also has an enormous oil wealth, more than enough to enrich itself and not Russia, having common borders not only with Russia, but with North Ossetia, Ingushetia (South Ossetia, not acknowledged by the mainstream interpretation of International Law, but acknowledged by Russia and a few other states as a country and also the subject of debated acknowledgement), Georgia and Dagestan, all more or less strategically important to Russia. Thus, International Law

A T-64 of the armed forces of the self-proclaimed Donetsk People's Republic, seen in May 2023. (Russian social media)

was created in a way to not allow "substantial" self-determination, unless self-determination fully complies with the constitution of the majority nation, also including the laws of the majority nation. There is no way that Moscow and the majority of Russia would allow substantial (radical) self-determination by Chechnya in order to allow it to become a fully independent nation state, unless a civil war or a powerful 'colour revolution' took place, bringing to power yet unknown political forces, probably loyal to the West.

Whom was Wagner fighting in Ukraine?

Originally, in 2014–2015, Wagner Group PMC in Ukraine fought four types of military formations: the Ukrainian Armed Forces (ZSU) and the Ukrainian National Guard,[42] and armed formations of foreign and Ukrainian volunteers that were more or less under the control of the ZSU.[43]

> Now that the Azov Battalion has been decimated, the Krakens stand to become Ukraine's most famous band of volunteers — and arguably most controversial, like their Azov brethren. Critics said both have drawn fighters from ultranationalist and far-right groups, an allegation their soldiers reject as Russian propaganda.[44]

Whenever neo-Nazism in Ukraineis mentioned, the authors are well aware of the fact that Russia publicly maintains a neo-Nazi regime at home, while being one of the few countries in the world that damns Ukrainian neo-Nazis and declares this issue to be important. This conclusion is important explaining certain official positions of the Kremlin, i.e., when the meaning of 'de-Nazification' is explained as one of the main official goals of the Russian 'Special Military Operation' in Ukraine.[45] Kyiv flatly rejects as Russian propaganda the idea that neo-Nazis are fighting on its side. In the international community the issue of neo-Nazism in Ukraine is either not raised or is considered to be controversial.[46]

However, since most soldiers and leaders of Wagner are Russian, it makes sense to call things the way Russians believe is right in order get an insight of Wagner's motivations, rather than sweeping the whole issue under the carpet, by calling them 'far-right elements' and nothing else. We acknowledge that there are all sorts of far-right elements in Russia, as there are in Ukraine: some are not neo-Nazis at all, some have strange and historically outdated mindsets of classic Nazim, daring to wear classic *Schutzstaffel* (SS) symbols from the era of the Second World War, some are partially influenced by Nazi ideas, somewhat adapted to our era, using modified Nazi symbols, or brand-new ones, when their connection to Nazism is clear, but could endlessly be debated.

The authors would argue, that ultra-nationalist and far-right tendencies[47] might not help the cause of the freedom of the Ukrainian nation state, no matter whether called Russian propaganda[48] or not: 'Critics said both [the Azov and Kraken battalions] have drawn fighters from ultranationalist and far-right groups, an allegation their soldiers reject as Russian propaganda.'[49] Far-right elements pose a national security risk in any societies that consider themselves democratic. Far-right elements generate highest risks of classic war crimes and all sorts of human rights abuses if they become members of armed groups, no matter whether they are formally integrated into government structures on paper, or not. In Ukraine, they are formally integrated into government structures, but it is disputable to what extent that might 'tie their hands'. Human rights abuses can be committed by the state (or particular state structures, such as secret services or the police) and also by far-right elements, who are not the only possibly violent criminal layer of a society. Human rights abuses could be committed against civilians, or against armed personnel (such as soldiers or policemen). They can be committed against own personnel, or personnel of another state. It is hard to name all possible human rights violations, but they stretch from violent acts against differently thinking groups such as LGBTQ, ethnic minorities (such as Russians or Roma in Ukraine), and those suspected of collaboration with the enemy (in the case of Ukraine it is Russia). Human rights abuses stretch from threats of violence to torture, sexual harassment or abuse, to rape, extrajudicial executions, and forced disappearances, for example.

Without accusing any parties of the Ukraine war at this time, in general, the following can be said to be true:

- All major wars are accompanied by war crimes, especially if the war is somehow interrelated with a civil war, such as the war in Ukraine.
- Twenty-first century wars make no exceptions concerning the emergence of war crimes.
- War crimes are usually committed on both sides, and not by one or the other party exclusively.
- 'Own' war crimes are usually not 'advertised', but rather kept secret and/or denied, or at least downplayed.
- 'Enemy' war crimes are usually widely propagated ('advertised') and tend to be exaggerated.
- The issue of human rights abuses is usually over-politicised in wartime, when the parties use it as a tool to discredit the enemy and gain sympathy for their own side.
- Armed far-right elements are dangerous, because when it comes to violence, they feel ready to commit acts that people with balanced views would not do, or at least struggle with their consciousness, moral dilemmas prior to committing human rights abuses or war crimes.

For such reasons, when far-right units play a key role in the defence of a country, there is 'something deeply wrong going on somewhere': 'A far-right battalion has a key role in Ukraine's resistance. Its neo-Nazi history has been exploited by Putin'.[50]

Far-right units and elements are counterproductive, if Russian public opinion is taken into consideration, as a whole, since it stimulates wide layers of the Russian population to agree to fight ferociously against this phenomenon. For historic reasons, the Russian population tend to be sensitive to issues of neo-Nazism, and that of similar far-right world views and practices. Many Russian families still have survivors from the Second World War, or ancestors no longer alive but still vivid in the memories of their Russian relatives, who either fought the war on the Soviet (Russian) side or suffered much due to the war as civilians. Furthermore, Ukrainian neo-Nazi and far-right tendencies and practices supply the Russian politicians and ideology makers with evidence necessitating the continuation of the 'Special Military Operation'. Far-right and neo-Nazi armed entities cause hatred and unnecessary injuries between ethnic groups, and that hits back in the long run, especially between Ukrainians and Russians, since they not only live in neighbouring countries, but due to the fact that there is still a significant Russian minority in Ukraine that is probably still the most numerous ethnic minority there. The organisation of far-right nationalist elements in Ukraine into military units, and providing them with military training and equipment was one of the biggest mistakes since 2014, a huge national security breach, and a recipe for classic war crimes, such as repressions against politically opposing forces, such as pro-Russian civilians.

Above: A cargo version of the Chekan mine-protected ambush resistant (MRAP) vehicle, and a BM-21 multiple rocket launcher of the Wagner Group, seen in February 2023. By that time the mercenary group were well-equipped with such heavy equipment. (via Dean O'Brien)

Right: Two of Wagner Group's mercenaries on the streets of Soledar in early 2023. (Grey Zone)

2
BATTLE OF BAKHMUT

Following its clandestine involvement in Ukraine in 2014–2015, the Wagner Group was slow to re-emerge on the scene once the Russian Federation launched its all-out invasion on 24 February 2022.[1] Indeed, Telegram channels associated with Wagner claimed that the PMC began mobilising for its renewed deployment in Ukraine only during March 2022, and that the first battalion tactical group (BTG) of 700 combatants arrived from Africa on the 19th of that month. Wagner documentation captured and analysed by the Ukrainian online platform Mediazona in 2024 however, revealed that the mercenaries were involved in the first weeks of Putin's all-out invasion, and had suffered nearly 300 casualties before the Battle of Popasna, starting in April 2022 (see below for details).

The large-scale involvement of Wagner began only in mid-March when, in the aftermath of the above-mentioned, massive Russian losses during attempted advances on Kyiv, Chernihiv and Sumy, and the resulting withdrawals from those parts of Ukraine, Yevgeny Prigozhin was spotted in the Russian-occupied Donbas again. Over the following two weeks, rumours began making circles that Wagner PMC was recruiting Libyan and Syrian nationals for service in Ukraine. By the end of March 2022, the MOD in Moscow also assigned the group control over several extremist paramilitary groups in Russia, including the Russian Imperial Legion and the neo-Nazi Russich Group. Combined with up to 1,000 foreigners – including not only Libyans and Syrias, but also Iraqi nationals – these formed the first two BTGs of Wagner PMC in Ukraine in 2022.

Each of the two BTGs consisted of headquarters and two fully equipped companies, although they still lacked heavy weapons. They made their presence felt for the first time in the Popasna area, in early April, when their commanders organised a three-wave attack on local Ukrainian positions. The first wave included units staffed by Ukrainian separatists, who were tasked with spotting Ukrainian positions and minefields; they were followed by regulars of the 150th Motor-Rifle Division and the 155th Naval Infantry Brigade. Wagner mercenaries were in the third wave, while troops of the 76th VDV Division and the 90th Tank Division were waiting for their opportunity to exploit. Overall aim of the operation was the destruction of the Ukrainian 24th Mechanised Brigade and a breakthrough of the front line with the aim of reaching Bakhmut, Kramatorsk and Sloviansk, where the assailants were expecting to meet Russian units advancing from Izyum and Lyman, thus encircling the concentration of Ukrainian forces deployed in Severodonetsk and Lysychansk.[2]

Following two days of heavy air strikes and massive artillery barrages aimed at the positions of one of the battalions of the 24th Mechanised Brigade, on 4 April the Russians launched their onslaught along the railway line from Pervomaiske into Popasna. Next, the mercenaries began clearing the town using classic tactics of urban warfare: they would first advance along two parallel roads before mopping up the area in between. Although hopelessly outnumbered and under constant and massive pressure from the Russian artillery, the Ukrainians defended bitterly and continued causing heavy losses. During the night from 19 to 20 April, they ambushed a 25-man assault team from Wagner PMC consisting of Libyans and Syrians. In another case, they called-in a strike by Turkish-made Bayraktar TB.2 unmanned aerial vehicles and hit the headquarters of the separatist

A Wagner mercenary in a typical pose in front of the badly damaged Cultural Palace, in the centre of Bakhmut, in late May 2023. (via Dean O'Brien)

A view of downtown Bakhmut in late May 2023, from the square with the City Hall and the Cultural Palace towards the two famous, semi-circular buildings at the junction of Svobody and Miru Streets. (via Dean O'Brien)

4th Motor-Rifle Brigade, killing over 50 separatist, Russian and mercenary officers. It was thus only on 20 April that the involved Russian forces managed to break through north-east of the town. This success was rather short-lived: not only did Ukrainian reinforcements arrive in time to prevent a collapse of their front lines, but they continued resisting with such success that it took Wagner's 'Musicians' until 7 May to clear Popasna and declare its ruins as secured for Russia.

As well as recruiting from veteran FSB, GRU, and VDV operators, at this time Wagner PMC was granted official permission to start recruiting within the ranks of former pilots and ground personnel of the Russian Aerospace Force (VKS). Eventually, enough of these had been contracted to staff a squadron of the 266th Assault Aviation Regiment equipped with Sukhoi Su-25 close support aircraft. This was of particular importance because this unit, and two others of the VKS operating the type, suffered significant losses early during the invasion and were short of experienced pilots. The presence of mercenary pilots became clear on 30 April 2022 when the Ukrainian air defences shot down the Su-25 piloted by Colonel (ret.) Nikolai Markov, killing him. This 67-year-old veteran from Belarus had been serving with Wagner in Africa since around 2015. Later in 2022, the Wagner Group was also able to recruit enough pilots and ground personnel to man a squadron equipped with Sukhoi Su-24M fighter-bombers of an unknown regiment of the VKS.

With the seizure of Popasna neither resulting in a collapse of the Ukrainian front line, nor in withdrawal from Severodonetsk and Lysychansk, the Russians organised a new, even more massive effort. In coordination with crossing attempts over the Siversky Donets River from the north, from the direction of Lyman and Torske, between 9 and 11 May 2022, they launched another three-wave assault to take the villages of Oleksandropillia and Komyshuvakha, south-west of Lysychansk, and then attempted cutting off the T1302 road – the primary supply route of the Ukrainian garrisons, from the south. Although both villages were eventually secured by Wagner, amid fierce resistance and heavy losses, the mercenaries, the 76th VDV Division and the 90th Tank Division were

An overhead view of a T-72B, assigned to the 150th Motor-Rifle Division, knocked out while supporting an assault by the Wagner Group in the Popasna area on 24 May 2022. (ZSU)

Yevgeny Prigozhin, seen at the time of his semi-secret re-appearance in Donbass, eastern Ukraine, in late March 2022. (Grey Zone/Wagner PMC)

slow to exploit: they were stopped after seizing Volodymyrivka and Nova Kamyanka.³

The reason for the repeated failures of the 'Musicians' to achieve an operational breakthrough for the Russian armed forces was their lack of heavy weaponry. Therefore, while the two original BTGs of the Wagner Group continued their involvement in the battles for Severodonetsk and Lysychansk, the next three formations staffed by mercenaries were organised and equipped in significantly reinforced form. Drawing upon their own experiences from Libya, and the experiences of formations controlled by the Islamic Revolutionary Guards Corps in Syria, and with extensive help from the MOD in Moscow, the new BTGs of the 'Musicians' consisted of two or three infantry companies each, but accompanied by at least as large a fire-support element, including 120mm mortars, snipers, anti-tank guided missiles, artillery pieces (mainly old 122mm D-30 howitzers), multiple rocket launchers (BM-21s), infantry fighting vehicles (like BMP-2s and -3s), main battle tanks (primarily T-80s drawn from reserve stocks), and Pantsir S1 short-range air defence systems (ASCC/NATO reporting name 'SA-22 Greyhound').

Above: Wreckage of 'Bunny', probably the most famous Ukrainian tank. This T-80BVM was captured in March 2022 by the Ukrainian 93rd Mechanised Brigade in the outskirts of Kharkiv and upgraded through addition of new ERA armour on the sides. Gauging by the 'kill rings' on its gun barrel and claims of the crew, it destroyed at least six Russian tanks (including the only T-80UM2 in Russian service). In Bakhmut, it was immobilised by fire from a 240mm mortar: the crew set it on fire while abandoning the vehicle. (via Dean O'Brien)

Left: A destroyed Russian T-72 or T-90 main battle tank behind a completely ruined apartment building. (via Dean O'Brien)

The crew of a Wagner-operated BMP-3 infantry fighting vehicle seen in Ukraine in the summer of 2022. (Wagner PMC/Grey Zone)

By early June 2022, Wagner PMC had three BTGs in Ukraine, including one in Severdonetsk, one (the 1st Tactical Group) west of Popasna, and one (the 2nd Tactical Group) in the Svitlodarsk area. However, the process of working up additional units was rudely interrupted on 10 June 2022 when the Ukrainians hit a football stadium in Kadiivka (known as 'Stakhanov' in Russian), in the Russia-controlled Luhansk Oblast, with at least one, but possibly up to three, OTR-21 Tochka tactical ballistic missiles (ASCC/NATO reporting name 'SS-21 Scarab'). The facility was used as a base for the first big Wagner BTG and the strike reportedly caused between 250 and 300 casualties. This was one of the reasons why the Russians managed to start their final offensive on Severodonetsk only about a week later, when the fourth of the Wagner BTGs became involved in an assault on the heavily fortified village of Zolote, south of Lysychansk.[4]

While all assaults on Zolote failed, the southernmost mercenary BTG was more successful. On 13 June, attacking from Ilovaisk and Vidrodzhennya, it breached the Ukrainian front line along the M03 highway in the Svitlodarsk area and secured Versyhna. This success not only forced the Ukrainians to fall back on Zaitseve, Traveneve, and Dolomitne, but also secured the stretch of the highway connecting Popasna with Horlivka, significantly improving the Russian logistics as result. That said, it took the mercenaries more than three weeks longer to force the ZSU to withdraw from the well-fortified compound of the Vuhlehirske Tes power plant, a few kilometres west of Svitoldarsk.

Following a series of costly failures, in mid-June 2022 the Russians reorganised their formations in the area south of Lysychansk and combined three Wagner BTGs with the remnants of several separatist regiments. Initially, these conducted diversionary attacks on ZSU positions in the Klynove area before, on 21 June, assaulting via Toshkivka in the north, and via Vryubivka in the south. Once

On 18 June 2022, Wagner's 'flying component' suffered its second known loss. While supporting another mercenary attempt to break through to the T1302 road, the Su-25 piloted by Andrei Vladimirovich Fedorchukov was shot down by troops of the 72nd Mechanised Brigade of the ZSU, and the pilot captured. This photograph shows Fedorchukov in Ukrainian captivity. (ZSU)

Wreckage of the football stadium in Kadiivka, hit on 10 June 2022 by at least one Ukrainian tactical ballistic missile while used as a headquarters of the Wagner Group in Luhansk Oblast. (Russian social media)

again, the separatists leading these attacks suffered extensive losses. However, the following 'Musicians' of the 1st Tactical Group managed to break through and secure Myrna Dolyna, then entered Vovchoyrivka, and by 23 June, approached Verknokamyanka and Topolivka. With this, the Ukrainian hold on both Severodonetsk and Lysychansk, as well as on the fortifications in Zolote and Hirske, became untenable and the ZSU initiated a general withdrawal via Bilohorivka towards Siversk. By 1 July, the Ukrainians evacuated their troops from Severodonetsk and were in the process of withdrawing from Lysychansk as well: supported by Spetsnaz of the GRU, one of the Wagner BTGs then followed up by crossing the Siversky Donets and securing the village of Pryvillia. Three days later, the 'Musicians' seized Verkhnokamyanka, thus ending the three-month-long battles for Severodonetsk and Lysychansk with success. That said, the Russian claims that they had encircled and captured '2,000 nationalists' were wildly exaggerated: the ZSU lost about 2,000 killed and up to 10,000 injured – but over the course of three months, and most of these while forced to evacuate across open fields between Lysychansk and Bilohorivka, exposed to both direct and indirect Russian fire.[5]

Battle of Bakhmut

If there was one major clash that symbolised the involvement of the Wagner Group in the war in Ukraine then this was the Battle of Bakhmut fought from July 2022 until May 2023. Ironically, the showdown over the town known as Artemivsk in Russia, with a pre-war population of about 70–80,000, was almost exclusively motivated by the illusions of the top leaders in Kyiv and Moscow. For his part, Putin was determined to clearly demonstrate his resolve to destroy Ukraine. Considering the fact that through June and July the Western allies of Ukraine began providing heavy armament and ammunition to Kyiv, Putin and his top military commanders were also in a rush to break the ZSU before it could grow into a force with the potential to defeat the Armed Forces of the Russian Federation (VSRF) on the battlefield. Correspondingly, Russian claims that the place was predominantly populated by Russians were ignored, and both the artillery of the VSRF and the air power of the VKS were given a 'free hand' to 'erase' not only the local factories, but any man-made structures. As in Chechnya in the early 2000s, and then in Mariupol during February–May 2022, the destruction of the town was expected to serve as a warning to the rest of Ukraine as to what would happen if it did not capitulate. That said, the 'victories' in Izyum, Kremina, Rubizhne, Popasna, Severodonetsk, and Lysychansk had completely exhausted the peacetime Russian ground forces with which the invasion was initiated: the majority of slightly over 190 BTGs that were originally deployed and staffed by contract personnel was decimated to the degree where fewer than 100 were still inside Ukraine during the summer of 2022: the remaining manoeuvre units were critically short of infantry, and the mass of their main battle tanks crewed by only two, instead of the standard three, men. In similar fashion, the 'meat' of the Russian invasion of eastern Ukraine – units of the self-declared Luhansk and Donetsk people's republics – had suffered such losses in early assaults over the old Line of Control, in Mariupol, and especially during the battles for Severodonetsk and Lysychansk, that they had to be refilled with reservists from Russia. While selected other assets – mainly those of the VDV and Spetsnaz – were still largely intact, Moscow was reluctant to deploy its meagre intervention forces.

Therefore, not only Putin and his Minister of Defence, Shoygu, but even the Chief of the General Staff of the VSRF, Gerasimov, accepted the idea of the Wagner Group fighting this battle. This promised to buy the time necessary for the regular forces to be refilled with mobilised reservists at a rate of 25,000-30,000 a month. Obviously, the mercenary organisation was much too small for this task: indeed, despite its continuously growing popularity at home and abroad, the number of volunteers it was attracting remained insufficient. Therefore, the idea was born to bolster the Wagner PMC through recruiting convicts from prisons and penal colonies around Russia instead. Incorporating the first groups of these, by August 2022, the number of Wagner BTGs deployed in Ukraine grew to seven.

On the other hand, the President of Ukraine, Volodimir Zelensky fell for his own illusions as well. Based on experience from February–March 2022, he was convinced that the West was ready to bolster supplies of armament and ammunition only if the Ukrainians could 'demonstratively fight and resist'. Because he was aiming to obtain enough aid to launch a major counteroffensive that would break the VSRF and liberate large parts of occupied territories with a single blow, in the case of Bakhmut, he ordered the ZSU to buy time through accepting the battle and fighting the Russian onslaught,

Army General Valery Geasimov (left), Chief of the General Staff of the Russian Armed Forces since 2012, with General Sergey Surovikin, the commander of all Russian forces in Ukraine since summer 2022. As of June 2023, Surovikin was reportedly 'representing the interests' of the Wagner Group in the Ministry of Defence in Moscow. (Russian Ministry of Defence)

regardless the losses. This decision found no understanding within the top ranks of the Ukrainian armed forces, which preferred a gradual withdrawal to Chasiv Yar, a town about 20 kilometres further west positioned atop a dominant elevation and well-fortified. Hesitantly, but nevertheless, the Commander-in-Chief of the ZSU, Valery Zaluzhny accepted Zelensky's order.

The Wagner Group began its operations against Bakhmut around 6 July 2022, when – in cooperation with GRU Spetsnaz – it began infiltrating the village of Klynove, about 15 kilometres south-east of the industrial zone of Soledar, and 10 kilometres east of Bakhmut. A simultaneous push by the 2nd Tactical Group in the direction of the Vuhlehirska power plant encountered bitter resistance though: indeed, a local counterattack by a battalion of the Ukrainian 30th Mechanised Brigade not only caused severe losses to the mercenaries, but nearly collapsed a sector of the Russian front line in the Vershyna area.

After withdrawing east of Vershyna and stabilising their front line with help of Spetsnaz troops, the 2nd Tactical Group resumed its offensive operations a few days later. Indeed, infiltration attempts into Klynove gradually grew into ever bigger assaults, which went on for days without any tangible results – partially because the 30th Mechanised had now been reinforced by elements of the 72nd Mechanised Brigade equipped, amongst other items, with British-supplied FV103 Spartan armoured personnel carriers. Nevertheless, the 2nd Tactical Group – always proceeded by separatist formations – continued assaulting and eventually prevailed: by August it secured Klynove and reached the village of Vesela Dolyna and the southern fringes of Opytne (the southern suburb of Bakhmut). Briefly interrupted by another Ukrainian HIMARS strike on one of the forward headquarters of the Wagner group – this time on 14 August, when the quarters in Popasna, on Mironivska Street 12 was completely destroyed – the onslaught was reinforced in early September by when decimated separatist units were replaced by assault formations staffed by convicts. By sending these into up to 15–20 successive attacks against selected Ukrainian positions every single day, the 'Musicians' took the ZSU by surprise and by mid-September secured not only Vuhlehirska power plant (losing 58 troops in the process), but also Zaitseve, Odradivka, and Kodema. From there, Wagner began pushing into Opytne in the north, and around the southern side of Klishchivka towards Kurdyumivka, with the aim of finding a suitable site to cross the Siversky Donets – Donbas Canal, and thus start encircling the Ukrainian garrison in Bakhmut.

A propaganda photograph from September 2022, when Moscow was not too proud to announce the 'return' of Wagner to Ukraine. (Russian social media)

A still from a video showing a Wagner mercenary describing one of the sharp, close-range clashes with troops of the 30th Mechanised Brigade of the ZSU, near Vuhlehirska power plant, in mid-September 2022. (Russian social media)

The Meat Grinder

Wagner's 'official' start of the 'Bakhmut Meat Grinder' was on 8 October 2022, when the group began assaulting Kurdyumivka, south of Bakhmut: while managing to encircle and force into surrender a company of the ZSU, capturing up to 40 enemy troops in the process, 30 Wagner combatants were killed on just the first day, for a total of 965 since the actual start of the battle. The PMC continued assaulting the village until securing it on 29 November, by when it had lost 3,605 mercenaries and convicts killed. By then, the total number of personnel under the control of Wagner was widely estimated at 50,000, of whom about 10,000 were contractors and at least 40,000 pardoned convicts.

By that time, most of Wagner's tactical groups had been reorganised into assault detachments: the core of each included a group of mercenaries or GRU Spetsnaz, a UAV group, an engineer squad, and an evacuation group: their primary manoeuvring elements were some 5–8 assault groups, all staffed by convicts and each including a rifle squad, reinforced by a grenade launcher and a flamethrower crew. Each assault group was supported by a single tank, sometimes one or two infantry fighting vehicles, a platoon of 82mm or 120mm mortars, and one D-30 howitzer. Usually, one assault detachment would be tasked with operations for about 24 hours: then it would be withdrawn for rest and reorganisation lasting some 24–48 hours, while replaced by another assault detachment. Their attacks were usually followed by 'regular' Wagner BTGs, the task of which was to secure and expand the position that was reached. In this fashion, the Wagner Group was capable of keeping the targeted ZSU units under near constant pressure.

Such assaults were conducted against the Ukrainian defences of Bakhmut through all of November 2022: the 'Musicians' would send two or three of their assault groups to attack, have them chopped to pieces, then they would follow with another wave. Rather unsurprisingly, reports soon emerged about the mercenary group suffering huge losses, frequently up to 200 mercenaries and convicts a day. The situation began to change only around 27 November, when the Wagner Group refocused on attacking the southern side of Soledar, and into the southern side of Opytne. Several times, the Russians managed local breakthroughs and a number of smaller ZSU units had to be saved by counterattacks. Eventually, in a matter of five days, the Ukrainians lost more than 50 square kilometres of terrain south of Bakhmut, and the Wagner Group then refocused on assaulting Klishchivka. While a small village with a pre-war population of just 200, this was bitterly contested, because it was on the approach to a hill with a major Ukrainian fortification atop it, and – perhaps more importantly – also one dominating the local stretch of the Siversky Donets-Donbas Canal. On 2 December

PROJECT 42174[6]

The codename for recruitment of prisoners by Wagner was 'Project 42174'. The process of recruiting them, and the offer made by the Wagner Group, were relatively simple. Starting from 1 July 2022, at Yablonevka IK7 in Leningrad Oblast, either Prigozhin in person or his teams of recruiters would visit a colony, gather the convicts and propose a deal to them: six months at the front in exchange for a pardon and complete erasure of criminal records, along with monetary allowances and insurance payouts to the family in case of death or severe injury. The convicts were given 'five minutes' to make their choice. Those who accepted were interviewed and vetted by Wagner's representatives, evaluated for their physical condition, and allocated to the 'Umbrella' detachment. They were brought to training camps in Luhansk Oblast (for example in the Polar Wolf supermax colony in the village of Kharp), trained for two weeks and assigned to assault detachments.

Following initial success in prisons and penal colonies in western Russia, Prigozhin and several teams of his recruiters moved rapidly towards the east. After visiting Nizhny Novgorod, Karelia, Novgorod, and Pskov in July, through August they reached Komi, then went to central Russia (Tula, Ryazan, Tver, Kaluga, and Vladimir regions), before focusing on the south-west (Rostov, Voronezh, Belgorod) in September 2022. In October, they reached the areas beyond the Urals, and by December were already recruiting in the Far East. In 2022, inmates from 74 'medium-security' colonies and 28 'super maximum security' colonies were recruited by the Wagner Group, with Prigozhin repeatedly stressing he was seeking murderers and robbers to join his PMC. Through 2023, recruiters also went to four medical prison facilities and seven penal settlements.

Andrey Troshev (left), Wagner's top commander for operations in Ukraine. (Wagner PMC)

Wagner operatives took great care to distribute people from the same prison to very different units, which is why nearly everybody lost contact with prisoners they used to know, and many of their subsequent stories are next to impossible to reconstruct. What is certain is that the majority of prisoners recruited by Wagner participated in 'meat assaults' in the Bakhmut area and this is where nearly all of them died, too. The first known fatality amongst the convicts occurred on 15 July 2022, when a prisoner from Yablonevka with the call-sign 'Polsaty' ('Striped') was killed.

Project 42174 was terminated in February 2023. Prigozhin's press service declared that the related decision was 'beyond his competence'. With hindsight, it is certain that the Ministry of Defence in Moscow made the decision to continue recruiting convicts on its own.

Prigozhin (wearing civilian clothes, in the centre), addressing the inmates of a Russian prison in the autumn of 2022. (Wagner PMC)

2022, while supporting efforts to repel a ZSU counterattack there, Wagner's fliers suffered their third known loss, when a Su-24M crewed by Alexander Sergeyevich Antonov and Vladimir Nikolaevich Nikishin was shot down. Nevertheless, and after the place changed hands some three or four times, the Russians managed to secure Klishchivka.

The Wagner Group experienced another setback on 11 December, when its new headquarters in Kadivka was demolished by a strike from a US-made and Ukrainian-operated M142 HIMARS: the number of casualties from that attack remains unknown. What is certain is that the mercenary commanders reacted by attempting something different: starting from 13 December and supported by the GRU Spetsnaz and 31st Guards VDV Brigade, they attempted to seize the eastern side of Bakhmut through an all-out assault. Amid massive casualties – including the loss of 27 different armoured fighting vehicles and the death of 258 combatants on a single day (for a total of 5,258 since the start of the battle) – they did manage to reach Patrice Lumumba Street. Nevertheless, this proved to be the limit of their achievement, either because around this time the VSRF artillery began experiencing shortages of ammunition, or because the Ministry of Defence in Moscow, concerned about the growing popularity of the Wagner Group with the Russian public, refused to supply the demanded amounts. As a result, the Wagner Group proved unable to demolish selected Ukrainian positions to the desired level.

A still from a video showing troops of the K-2 Battalion of the Ukrainian 54th Motorised Brigade inspecting bodies of Wagner combatants following one of their assaults on eastern Bakhmut in mid-December 2022. According to the same video, six dead Wagner combatants were found at this spot: the bodies of more than 60 others lay nearby. (54th Motorised Brigade, ZSU)

Ruins of the Wagner HQ in Kadivka, seen following the HIMARS strike of 11 December 2022. (via Iullia Mendel)

An aerial view of eastern Bakhmut during a Ukrainian counterattack in mid-December 2022. (ZSU)

Soledar

With the failure of the big push into eastern Bakhmut coming atop months in which Moscow delivered nothing but retreats, the Wagner commanders changed their tactics again, and on 16 December launched assaults into Yakovlivka and Pidhorodne: the former was a village north-east of Soledar, and the later in the north-eastern outskirts of Bakhmut. The aim was to outflank the defences of Soledar while driving a wedge between the ZSU positions in that area and those in northern Bakhmut. Rushing assault teams of former prison inmates across barren fields, now full of mud, shell craters, and decomposing bodies, the effort initially ended in severe casualties. Moreover, a series of Ukrainian counterattacks conducted on 18 and 19 December, forced the assailants out of both Yakovlivka and Pidhorodne, and also out of southern Opytne.

According to unconfirmed reports from unofficial sources in Russia, at that point in time, even the General Staff of the Russian Armed Forces in Moscow was on the brink of ordering Wagner to abandon its attempts to seize Bakhmut. On the contrary, convinced he was right, and aiming to strengthen his hand against what he termed with 'corrupt and incompetent generals in Moscow', Prigozhin was determined to continue. What came to his aid was a piece of intelligence indicating the decision of the General Staff in Kyiv to withdraw the exhausted 128th Mountain Assault Brigade from Soledar, and replace it with the relatively inexperienced (but largely British-trained) 46th Airborne Brigade, between 26–28 December. The area around Soledar included large salt mines (prior to the all-out invasion of 2022, these were operated by Artemsil, the biggest producer of salt in Europe), and huge sources of gypsum. The resulting network of tunnels enabled the 128th to rapidly move troops from one side of its fortifications to the other, entirely unobserved by the Russians, but also to avoid the bulk of the artillery fire and air strikes directed at its positions. Therefore, although the town was razed to the ground by repeated Russian air strikes and artillery barrages that had targeted it since May 2022, its defences were still intact.

The onslaught on Soledar was initiated on 27 December: several volleys from TOS-1 multiple rocket launchers caught the Ukrainians at the most inopportune moment: the 128th Brigade was already largely out of the town, but due to several mistakes amongst the commanders of the entire operation, the 46th Airborne Brigade was still in the process of deploying its troops to their new positions. As a consequence, a number of Ukrainian platoons were caught in the open and decimated. When this was followed by a mass assault of convicts from the south, one battalion of the 46th broke and ran. Reinforcements were rushed to the scene and the advancing Russians repeatedly hit by the 45th Artillery Brigade, however, by 1 January 2023, the convicts and mercenaries had not only entrenched themselves inside the ruins of the local sports centre: they were also approaching Blahodatne. Facing the threat of being cut off, the 46th Airborne Brigade was left with little choice but to fall back into the western side of Soledar. Arguably, the Russian success came at a price. While assaulting the centre of Soledar, on 6 January, one of Wagner's assault groups staffed by convicts is known to have been completely annihilated; in another, only three out of 35 combatants survived. Of course, neither anybody within Wagner, nor in Moscow cared about such facts.[7]

On 11 January – by when the Wagner Group is known to have lost 626 men in assaults against just Soledar (and a total of 8,323 since the start of the Battle of Bakhmut) – Prigozhin posed with a group of his mercenaries in what he claimed was one of the salt mines, and announced that the town had been completely captured. Actually, the Wagner PMC still had to do a great deal of fighting for Soledar – as made clear by the fact that on the next day it lost 213 mercenaries and convicts killed. At that point in time, it was the command echelons of the ZSU that made a series of mistakes, enabling a Russian victory: instead of deploying entire brigades to stabilise the front line, they attempted to patch up the situation by deploying battalions from very different units, most of which had never before trained or operated together. To make matters even more complex, both the commands in Kyiv and that responsible for Bakhmut repeatedly failed to coordinate the movements of their own units, and several times troops already under pressure from Russian assaults opened fire at units rushing forward to reinforce them. Amid the growing confusion, on 12 January 2023, even Kyiv was forced to confirm the loss of Soledar.

As subsequent developments were to show, this was also the beginning of the end of Bakhmut. That said, from Prigozhin's point of view, much more important was the fact that at the time the Ministry of Defence in Moscow was about to terminate his rights to continue recruiting from prisons (see the box about Project 42174) and claimed the seizure of the town for itself. Prigozhin was able to point out – publicly – that the first significant victory for Russia in nearly a year of this war, was a deed achieved by his company and its combatants.

Prigozhin posing with a group of his mercenaries, reportedly in one of Soledar's salt mines, on 11 January. Most likely, the photograph was actually taken in the caves of the Volodymyrivka area. (Grey Zone)

Left: Anton Olegovich Yelizarov, Wagner's top military commander during the battle of Soledar and, reportedly, successor to Prigozhin after the mutiny of June 2023. Sharing Prigozhin's history of crime, Yelizarov served with Wagner in Syria and Africa in 2015–2022, survived the mutiny of 2023 and subsequently signed a contract with the GRU's 'Afrika Korps', established in the aftermath of the Wagner mutiny. Reportedly, he was killed in Mali in July 2024. (Grey Zone)

Centre: A typical posed photograph of Wagner mercenaries taken at Sil train station, the westernmost point of Soledar, captured on 14–15 January 2023. (Yaremshooter)

Bottom: Three top commanders of Wagner BTGs, including Viktor Leonidovich 'Chief' Shevchuk (who served with Wagner in the Central African Republic and Libya since 2015), Andrey Nikolaevvich 'Lebed' Lebedev (former member of the Slavonic Corps PMC, then serving in Ukraine since 2014), and 'Dopusk' (a former convict who distinguished himself in combat and was promoted to lead one of the assault detachments), seen during a TV-interview with Putin's top propagandist, Vladimir Solovyev (first from left). (Russian social media)

A group of Wagner Group mercenaries in a typical pose, in the ruins of the hamlet of Sakko and Venzetti, north of Soledar, seized on 1 February 2023. (Wagner PMC)

Flanking Bakhmut

Parallel with the onslaught on Soledar, the Wagner Group was carrying out sustained attacks on the positions of the Ukrainian 24th Mechanised Brigade in Krasna Hora and Pidhorodne. This effort was almost as important as the seizure of Soledar, because it aimed not only to reach the road connecting the two places, but also the E40 highway, the primary supply link to Bakhmut. Indeed, by 8–9 January, the ferocity of assaults reached such a level, that the ZSU unit fell back on Paraskoviivka, Berkhivka, and northern Bakhmut. Realising the severity of the situation, the General Staff in Kyiv reacted by sending additional battalions from very different brigades to Bakhmut: by mid-January, elements from no fewer than 24 (possibly more) were fighting in the town. Unsurprisingly, this only increased the already growing chaos. Arguably, however, the Ukrainians were still launching effective counterattacks and, for example, on 13 January they recovered Klishchivka. However, by this time the disorganisation in their ranks was such that the Russians were able to quickly reorganise and seize the village back again four days later.[8]

Two Wagner mercenaries next to the badly damaged Vsesvyatsky Church, in downtown Bakhmut. (via Dean O'Brien)

Two burned-out BRDMs, the corpses of 7–8 Wagner operatives, and two survivors, seen while under Ukrainian shelling and attacks by 'first-person-view' (FPV) UAVs, outside Klishchivka, around 27–28 December 2022. (via Paul Javin)

On 25–26 January, the Wagner Group resumed its assaults north of Bakhmut: facing the uncoordinated defences of several Ukrainian battalions drawn from different brigades, its assault detachments managed to ford the Bakhmutska River and advance into Blahodatne, before turning south to enter Parskoviivka and Krasna Hora. Moreover, they collapsed the defences of a Ukrainian battalion defending the dominating elevations further west, and managed to reach the E40 highway north of the embattled town.

The Wagner Group has suffered such losses that the VSRF was forced to send several of its own units to bolster the positions in Bakhmut. Indeed, even the 106th VDV Division – a unit largely consisting of mobilised reservists – was deployed in the Klishchivka sector. Nevertheless, the detachments of mercenaries and convicts continued assaulting through February and March, eventually forcing the Ukrainians to withdraw into the western districts of the town in early April. By that point in time, Prigozhin had almost run out of convicts, in part because the Ministry of Defence in Moscow prevented Wagner from continuing to recruit more of them, while itself creating dozens of so-called 'Storm-Z' assault detachments staffed by inmates that volunteered to serve under same or similar conditions to those serving with the PMC. Hoping to complete 'his' operation, Prigozhin began openly, and ever more fiercely, attacking some of the top Russian commanders and the leadership of the defence industry.

In an attempt to continue pushing, the Wagner Group changed tactics again and began conducting nighttime assaults. These were usually conducted by assault groups of about 20 men, usually consisting of four subgroups: two were 'light' and armed only with personal firearms, while two were 'heavy', and armed with machine guns, grenade launchers and mortars or anti-tank weapons. The task of the light groups was to detect and initiate contact with the enemy; the heavy groups would then try to saturate the enemy position with their fire, pending follow-up assaults. Thanks to such improvements, by 18 February 2023, the Wagner PMC managed to fight itself deep into northern Bakhmut, and also into the villages of Dubovo-Vasylivka and Berkhivka, north-east of the town. Moreover, in the south, the mercenaries, convicts, and the 106th VDV Division not only seized Opytne, but also captured the 'Red Hill' above Klishchivka, and almost reached the centre of the town. With this, the ZSU garrison in Bakhmut was surrounded on three sides.

Arguably, the Wagner Group continued experiencing massive losses: according to its own documentation, 12,593 of its combatants were killed in the battle. Its commanders reacted with complete disregard for casualties: indeed, they imposed draconic disciplinary methods. Assault troops were prohibited from retreating without explicit orders, and any failure resulted in immediate execution. The evacuation of wounded personnel from the battlefield was prohibited until the assault had been successfully concluded, and any attempt to surrender resulted in summary execution. The combination of cruel and unscrupulous tactics, the fact that casualties amongst the convicts did not lessen the combat effectiveness of the command staff nor of weapons operators, and thus that of assault detachments, and additional mistakes by the top Ukrainian political and military leadership, were factors that contributed the most to the Group's ultimate success. For example, reconnaissance by fighting with small groups of infantry forced the Ukrainian positions to uncover themselves to the Russian drones: in turn, these were shelled heavily, and the repelling of one attack only resulted in attracting yet more enemy fire. It made no sense to try holding positions while they were exposed to constant assaults and shelling, because the 'Musicians' never ran out of troops, regardless of how many were killed while trying to approach. If this was not a problem enough, still failing to understand the futility of the entire effort, and falling for the illusion of the necessity to 'impress' the 'Western allies' of Ukraine, President Zelensky refused to permit an evacuation of the Ukrainian garrison: on the contrary, he continued ordering the ZSU to send additional reinforcements into Bakhmut even through March and April 2023, by when they were suffering heavy losses just trying to reach their destination along muddy minor roads connecting the town with the village of Ivanivske.

Sure enough, inside the town, the surviving Ukrainians continued fighting with grim determination and causing ever more massive losses to the Wagner Group. For example, by 23 March, by when the Russians had secured the centre and begun entering the western outskirts, the Russian documentation registered 15,933 mercenaries and convicts killed in action: about a month later, on 20 April, this figure had jumped to 17,788.[9] During this period, the Wagner Group began placing ever increased emphasis on the use of UAVs – primarily Mavic and Matrix – for reconnaissance and to monitor the activities of their assault groups. Unlike the VSRF and VDV, though, the mercenaries were using either US-made Motorola radios or the Chinese-made Baofeng walkie-talkies. The short range of such communication systems was typical of the constraints imposed by the limitations of Russian military communications in general – just like any damage or loss of drones usually meant the loss of effective control over the assault groups.

The Price of Success

Primarily at Zelensky's insistence, the battle of Bakhmut continued with the ZSU trying to hold out inside the western outskirts of the town into May of 2023. By then the situation of the Wagner Group was critical enough for the General Staff in Moscow to order additional reinforcements to the scene. The 7th VDV Division entered positions north of Soledar, the 137th VDV Brigade assumed the task of advancing along the E40 highway in the direction of Pryvillia, the 98th VDV Division joined the mercenaries and convicts inside the town, and the 106th continued pushing along the Siversk Donets-Donbas Canal, in the general direction of Chasiv Yar. Prigozhin was now regularly posting additional videos containing bitter complaints addressed to the top brass in Moscow. On 5 May – when 61 of his combatants were known to have been killed in combat (for a grand total of 18,537 since the start of the battle of Bakhmut) – he released a video of himself against a backdrop of a pile of bodies, while bitterly complaining about the failures of Shoygu and Gerasimov to support his operation. Two weeks later, he released another video, this time claiming that the Wagner PMC had captured Bakhmut.

When exactly the Battle of Bakhmut ended remains a topic of some dispute. On 20 May, by when the fighting was largely focused on the fields between the western side of the town and the nearby village of Ivanivske, Prigozhin released another video, claiming the capture of the town again. Kyiv acknowledged the loss 10 days later. That said, the battles went on for at least two weeks longer: the last three members of Wagner known to have been killed in this area fell on 5 or 6 June 2023. By then, after some 350 days of perhaps the most brutal fighting in this war, Prigozhin's private military company is known to have suffered the loss of 19,547 killed: 2,372 were contracted volunteers, while 17,175 were convicts. As far as is known, out of 48,000 recruited convicts, about 31,000 survived the Bakhmut Meat Grinder.

The number of Ukrainians killed during this showdown remains unknown. Prigozhin claimed that Wagner 'destroyed 50,000 ZSU fighters'. While understating his own losses by at least 50 percent, he specified that 50–70,000 Ukrainians were wounded. Moreover, he never discussed the losses suffered by GRU, VDV, and VSRF formations, which are known to have been at least 'significant'. For comparison, the independent online platform UALosses.org, counted a total of 5,501 members of the Ukrainian armed forces killed in Bakhmut between 15 July 2022 and 6 June 2023.

A Wagner mercenary atop one of the taller buildings in the centre of the completely ruined Bakhmut. (via Dean O'Brien)

Prigozhin in his famous video released on 5 May 2023, announcing the capture of Bakhmut from the roof of one of few high buildings left in the town. (Wagner PMC)

A still from a video showing a US-made M113 armoured personnel carrier, captured from the ZSU, in service with the Wagner Group during the Battle of Bakhmut in April 2023. (Wagner PMC)

Nearly all of the Wagner assaults into western Bakhmut during the final weeks of the battle were supported by extensive use of TOS-1 multiple rocket launchers with thermobaric warheads, and artillery bombardment employing incendiary ammunition. (RVvoenkory)

BLOOD MONEY

According to captured Wagner documentation analysed by Mediazona, the group paid 5,000,000 roubles (US$55,000) for every fallen mercenary or convict, plus 300,000 roubles (US$3,300) for a funeral (provided the latter was not organised by Wagner). During the group's involvement in Ukraine, Wagner is known to have paid 92,500,000,000 roubles (over US$1 billion) to relatives of recruited convicts, and 15,400,000,000 roubles (more than US$150 million) to the relatives of mercenaries. In other words, during the war in Ukraine, the PMC spent the staggering sum of 108,000,000,000 roubles (US$1.2 billion) on posthumous payments.

Prigozhin (right) and Yelizarov, seen in Soledar in early 2023. In a statement published in the Russian social media on 3 May 2023, Prigozhin announced that 'units of Wagner PMC advanced up to 230 metres and occupied an area of 54,000 square metres… 116 people from Wagner PMC died', before continuing to complain that while the Ukrainians 'have people and shells unlimited, the Ministry of Defence [in Moscow] does not issue artillery ammunition to us…. So far, there has been no reaction from the near-military officials, they ignore any questions from Wagner PMC.' (Wagner PMC)

3
MUTINY OF JUNE 2023

There were multiple warning signs prior to the armed mutiny by the Wagner Group on 23–24 June 2023 though they were not necessarily interpreted that way. Prigozhin's close relationship with the inner circle of the Russian elite around Putin, including the Russian president, together with his business and military successes – especially in Ukraine[1] – laid the foundations of his presidential ambitions. Following the Russian media, a feeling had often appeared that the Wagner Group had been the only serous player on the eastern front in Ukraine in 2023. Since the activities that Russia officially called their 'Special Military Operation' were considered to be a success by Moscow since the Wagner Group had a prominent role, the rise of Prigozhin to high level politics appeared to be inevitable. Prigozhin had already claimed that he intended to take part in the 2024 presidential elections in Russia.[2] However, this was highly unlikely to happen after the failed armed mutiny of the Wagner Group.

Prigozhin's military successes in Bakhmut had long been accompanied with quite detailed, passionate, and maybe even more importantly, publicly disclosed quarrels with the top Russian leadership of the Ministry of Defence. These often got out of hand and deeply disturbed the feelings of huge layers of Russian society. An outstandingly notorious example was the occasion when Prigozhin, fed up with the allegedly inadequate support of the Russian Ministry of Defence when supplying the Wagner Group in Ukraine, went as far as to publicly accuse of treason Army General Valery Gerasimov, the number one Russian general in the hierarchy, Chief of the General Staff of the Russian military and commanding general of the Special Military Operation in Ukraine. Furthermore, the gravity of the situation was increased by the fact that the public accusation was made on Russian Victory Day, 9 May 2023, and the substance of the accusation claimed, that General Gerasimov's aim was the extermination of the Russian people.[3]

> "Victory Day is the victory of our grandfathers, we did not deserve this victory by a millimetre. I have a paper in my hands, what we asked for, and what they are going to give us. There are 31 positions (types of items) in the request, of which the numbers that they give us are approximately 15. That is half" – claimed Prigozhin with an outrage. According to the businessman, today, May 9, Chief of the General Staff Valery Gerasimov corrected the figures and reduced the amount of ammunition to be provided by Wagner PMC. According to Prigozhin, this is a crime aimed at "genocide of the Russian people". And now the main task is to supply all the ammunition that is in the warehouses. We were promised on the 7th that they would give us. On the 8th, at two o'clock in the morning, a combat order was received, in which it was written "to give everything", he stressed.[4]

One might think, that Prigozhin's claims leading to a public quarrel with the Russian Ministry of Defence met a flat denial from the top Russian military leadership. However, it is not the case. Even President Putin acknowledged that the conflict between Wagner and the Russian Ministry of Defence had long existed, being resolved, case by case, by Putin himself.[5] It was also widely acknowledged, that such a quarrel should not have been part of the system.[6] Russian Army General Sergey Vladimirovich Surovikin, commander of the Aerospace Forces, also the commander of the 'Special Military Operation' in Ukraine between October 2022 and February 2023, appointed to be the key general responsible for coordination and cooperation with the Wagner Group in Ukraine, admitted the reluctance of the Russian Ministry of Defence to supply all military equipment that Wagner needed:

> General Sergei Surovikin, who was appointed by Defense Minister Sergei Shoigu as a link between PMC Wagner and the Russian Defense Ministry, commented on the situation. This is reported by the Telegram channel «Pool №3». According to Surovikin, from the very beginning of the Special Military Operation, he interacted with the head of the Wagner PMC on various issues and shared his opinion on the ongoing military operations. "From the very beginning, in the ministry, I opposed limiting the supply of weapons to them. I was limited to an extent as much as they could push it through, but now I have achieved this. I have achieved a concrete decision that will move our front forward. Yes, it cost a lot for me, but fortunately the train started moving. Shells are already being shipped and their production is increasing."[7]

It appeared highly likely that the problem of the Russian arms supply to Wagner in Ukraine was real. It is also likely that General Gerasiomov overrode the promises of General Surovikin and thus stalled the consensus between Surovikin and Prigozhin. However, it is quite debatable, whether the military supply needs of Wagner in Ukraine, presented by Prigozhin were justified or unrealistically inflated. One might argue that the Wagner Group was in the front line, performing the toughest defensive and offensive tasks, significantly contributing to the success of the Russian Armed Forces during the 'Special Military Operation'.[8] Very intense fighting at key parts of the Russian-Ukrainian front inevitably required more supplies than average, in particular ammunition, especially if the Ukrainian side sent newer and newer reserves to keep control of a part of the front, as it did in Bakhmut. Even Western mainstream sources acknowledged that the 'Ukrainians accepted Russian rules of the fighting':[9]

> Kyiv allowed itself to be drawn into the battle for Bakhmut on Russia's terms, losing the forces needed for the planned spring offensive, clinging stubbornly to a city with limited strategic options. Some of the military say that it makes sense to retreat to a new defensive line on the heights West of Bakhmut, while such a withdrawal can still be organized in a coordinated manner, while maintaining the combat capability of Ukrainian troops.[10]

In other words, based on Russian superiority in the air, artillery, air-defence and electronic warfare, it perfectly suited the Russians that the Ukrainian top political and military leadership sacrificed so many Ukrainian soldiers and their equipment when insisting that Bakhmut must be defended by the ZSU at all costs, thus 'constantly feeding' the Russian 'meatgrinder'. It was the Ukrainian President who insisted upon keeping Bakhmut, and Sirsky (Commanding General of the Ukrainian Army) supported the president's idea, ignoring military realities when loosing too much of their military capability.[11] However, the politicians could provide reasons in most of the cases, why enormous human sacrifices were in fact 'heroic' and 'necessary':

> Bakhmut, Zelenskiy said, is "hell." The ferocious defence of the Ukrainian forces has become another symbol of resistance and the country's unity, where the slogan "Bakhmut resists" has already been added to the mythology of the war. "The east is holding out because Bakhmut is fighting. This is the fortress of our morale. In fierce battles and at the cost of many lives, freedom is being defended here for all of us," Zelenskiy added.

It should be borne in mind that Bakhmut had already fallen into Russian hands, though denied by the Ukrainians for as long as possible, referring to some minor parts of the city, claimed to be under control of the Ukrainian Armed Forces, leading to questioning of the necessity of the enormous Ukrainian casualties sustained fighting Wagner.[12] Zelensky further claimed, that the loss of Bakhmut was the biggest failure of the United States of America since the war in Vietnam.[13]

The extremely bloody nature of the fighting for Bakhmut, admitted by Ukraine, Russia and third parties, partially as a result of the nature of urban warfare well covered by military manuals from around the world, could provide reasons why Wagner should get unlimited supplies of weapons and ammunition. However, in wartime it is very rare, that 'unlimited' supply could be provided, especially if the scale of the war is as great as in Ukraine, showing some similarities with the Second World War. It also needs to be kept in mind that the Russian Ministry of Defence was not only responsible for supplying Wagner but the entirety of the Russian Armed Forces as well. Some compromises would have had to be made providing a balance of costs and benefits. It could also be debated whether Gerasimov was sceptical when assessing Wagner's capabilities, or he wanted to weaken Wagner capabilities on purpose, as part of the struggle between the top Russian military leadership and the Wagner Group in Ukraine. It cannot be proven that Army General Gerasimov was purposefully downgrading Wagner's capabilities, thus inflicting more casualties on Wagner, than was ideal for the effective battle-fighting capability of the Russian PMC. However, it is a fact that several top generals of the Russian Ministry of Defence were against the huge growth of Wagner, even prior to its armed mutiny.

The publicly visible conflict between the Wagner Group and the Russian MOD was hard to interpret prior to the armed mutiny. Since it could be interpreted as a weakness of the entire Russian 'war machine', the question arises whether it was real or a fake. According to the initial judgement of the authors, even though there are strengths and weaknesses in the Russian warfighting system, much of the conflict between the Wagner Group and the Russian Ministry of Defence was 'exaggerated', thus a kind of deception to convince Kyiv to send more troops to challenge Russian forces, including the ongoing 'counteroffensive'. Being aware of the armed mutiny of the Wagner Group, the 'exaggerated' nature of the conflict between Wagner and the Russian Ministry of Defence is valid. However, retrospectively it was conducted not to convince the Ukrainians to challenge Russian forces more intensively, but rather as a result of the extreme and unjustified power ambitions of Prigozhin.

As Prigozhin claimed after the failed armed mutiny, his Wagner Group was supposed to hand over heavy equipment to the Russian military on 30 June 2023.[14] It proved to be true, since the Russian Ministry of Defence had earlier decided to make it mandatory to sign contracts with all volunteer armed formations, including PMCs, and a possible plan of handing over Wagner's heavy equipment by the end of June 2023 was a credible 'argument' to force Prigozhin to bow to the will of the Russian Ministry of Defence, which he had earlier categorically opposed. Should Prigozhin's claim to handover

A still from the famous video taken during the final stages of the Battle of Bakhmut, showing Prigozhin in front of a pile of bodies of Wagner combatants, while making fierce accusations against Shoygu and Gerasimov. (Wagner PMC)

heavy military equipment be true, Wagner was already on a path of decline from probably the world's strongest PMC to a limited elite force even prior to the failed armed mutiny. Such a historically imminent change of Wagner's status most likely added to Prigozhin's desperation to push ahead with the armed mutiny. It also shows that a top level Russian decision to disarm Wagner, approved by President Putin himself, had been made much earlier than during the failed mutiny or its immediate aftermath.

Armed Mutiny Against the Russian State or March of Equity?

In the evening of 23 June 2023, Prigozhin made several statements on social media, claiming that his bases had been bombarded by Russian forces, that the Russian Ministry of Defence denied. Later Prigozhin claimed, that he lost 30 soldiers as a result of the bombardment (not to be confused with Russian Aerospace Forces attacks on Wagner troops in Russian territory during the armed mutiny).[15] Most Russian experts considered Prigozhin's claims not credible, even though previous friendly fire incidents had been reported even in the Russian media,[16] leaving the audience to decide based on the pictures Prigozhin provided in social media. In theory, it is possible that Russian counterintelligence discovered the coming Wagner coup attempt, reported it to the Russian top leadership, and Putin made a decision to order a pre-emptive strike against those involved in the armed mutiny. However, this theory is unlikely to be true, not only because the Russian Ministry of Defence categorically denied it, but because such a limited strike is not credible and too weak to send a strong message to the potential mutineers.

Furthermore, while more than enough time has now passed to provide evidence of a bombardment,[17] such as the names of the casualties, or interviews with the relatives telling what happened, such evidence is still missing.[18]

Raids of 24 June 2023

Still organised in about a dozen assault detachments, according to Prigozhin's release to the Russian social media 25,000 of his troops began preparing for their operation in the evening of 23 June 2023, following a 'rocket strike by the Russian Ministry of Defence' that the boss of Wagner claimed 'killed dozens' of his combatants. He announced that he had held, 'a council of Wagner commanders', who decided to 'deal with the military leadership of Russia' and 'promised to destroy everyone who appears in their way'. Emphasising that his targets were Shoygu and Gerasimov, Prigozhin announced, 'Now Shoygu will not get away with just a resignation. But, he could be recording TikToks with his son-in-law in retirement in the United Arab Emirates.'

His commanders must have been busy with planning the coming operation for some time. This is clear from the fact that they managed to move multiple columns with nearly 1,000 military vehicles over the following 24 hours, and to keep these supplied. Just refuelling all the armoured fighting vehicles involved was something that could not be organised 'spontaneously'.

Upon being informed what they were about to do, many of the 'Musicians' began saying their farewells to their friends and relatives in the social media, while around 22.55hrs local time, Prigozhin – via the official Wagner Group channel in the Russian social media

Wagner mercenaries disarming a group of 'Akhmat Special Forces' – a group under the control of pro-Putin Chechen leader Ramazan Kadyrov, nominally subordinated to the Rosgvardiya – in the outskirts of Rostov-na-Donu, early on 24 June 2023. (Russian social media)

– issued a call for the Rosgvardia to join him: 'The most promising politician appeals to the National Guard [Rosgvardia] with an offer that is better not refused. Obeying criminal orders and attempting to interfere with the planned campaign of Justice will end badly for employees who have made the wrong choice.'

Only minutes later, Wagner units travelling in long convoys of military vehicles began moving out of their camps in Ukraine in an eastern direction along roads leading into south-western Russia. Shortly, Prigozhin announced via the Wagner Group's social media outlet that Gerasimov had ordered air strikes on his columns underway to Rostov-na-Donu (Rostov-on-Don), but the 'pilots refused to obey criminal orders'. One way or another, by this time the security services in Moscow had been put on alert and troops began deploying on the streets. However, no similar measures were initiated in any of the oblasts south of the capital: Prigozhin's account on the social-media platform v-kontakte was suspended, while the FSB began making telephone contact with Wagner combatants urging them not to make a mistake but to stop any use of force 'against the Russian people'. Finally, the FSB headquarters in Moscow announced: 'Prigozhin's statements and action amount to calls to start of an armed civil conflict on Russian territory and are a stab in the back for Russian servicemen fighting pro-fascist Ukrainian forces'.

In the north, at least three, possibly four assault detachments – reportedly including at least 400 military vehicles – drove into Voronezh and then secured the huge Buturlinovka Air Base (AB), where they shot down a transport aircraft variously identified as an Antonov An-24/26, an An-140, or an Ilyushin Il-114, reportedly 'full of troops'. Others meanwhile moved to the east, apparently attempting to reach Depot 375 Objekt C (controlled by the 12th Department of the Russian Ministry of Defence), outside Borisoglebsk: a storage facility for nuclear weapons. Another column simultaneously crossed the border into Belgorod Oblast. A few kilometres inside the Russian Federation, one of its Pantsir S1s opened fire at an Ilyushin Il-22M-11 airborne command post of the VKS. The aircraft that had taken-off from Ivanovo Severny AB, and was involved in operations against Ukraine, was hit and crashed outside Kantemirovka, in Voronezh Oblast, killing the crew of 10.

Further south, another assault detachment quickly secured Millerovo AB, before reaching the M-4 Highway, and then turning north towards Moscow, and ultimately, the two northernmost assault detachments started a race along the M-4 Highway in this direction. A few hours after leaving Buturlinovka, at least one of their columns came under several attacks by Sukhoi Su-34 fighter-bombers and Kamov Ka-52 attack helicopters of the VKS. The mercenaries returned fire with their Strela-10 (ASCC/NATO reporting name SA-13 'Gopher') self-propelled short-range surface-to-air missile systems, and shot down one Ka-52, killing its crew. Resuming their drive north, around noon their leading column passed Lipetsk, while around 18.00hrs local time, spearheads passed Tula and were approaching Kolomna, where the Rosgvardiya was establishing a defensive position across the M-4.

A BTR-82A of the 15,000-strong Derzhinsky Spetsnaz Division of the Rosgvardiya on the streets of Moscow, late on 23 June 2024. (Russian social media)

Although usually described as showing the downing of an Il-22M-11 airborne command post, these two stills from a video actually show an unidentified twin-engined transport aircraft (the Il-22 has four engines) shot down by Wagner troops as they approached Buturlinovka AB early on 24 June 2023. The exact type remains unknown. (Russian social media)

Above: Wreckage of the downed Il-22M-11, registration RF-75917. (ZSU)

Right: A Su-34 fighter-bomber passing low over the Buturlinovka area after attacking one of the Wagner Group's columns early on 24 June 2023. (Milinfolive)

A T-72 or T-90 main battle tank of one of Wagner's assault detachments being carried by a tilt-trailer truck along the M-4 Highway towards Moscow. (Russian Social Media)

In the south, at least three assault detachments advanced in different directions. Led by Fedor Leshchuk, the 7th drove for Novocherkassk, north-east of Rostov-na-Donu, near which was the major underground command facility of the Joint Strategic Command (OSK) South. Rumours circulated in the social media were that Gerasimov was there at the time, but that he narrowly avoided being arrested by Wagner.

Another assault detachment is known to have reached the M-4 highway in the Kozachi Tabory area, north of Rostov-na-Donu, before turning north, when it ran into a Rosgvardiya unit and brushed it aside in the course of a short firefight. This unit then seems to have opened fire at several VKS helicopters and is known to have shot down two Mil Mi-8MTRP-1 electronic warfare platforms and one Mil Mi-35 attack helicopter (the crews of the first two reportedly survived but a member of the third was killed).

Meanwhile, led by Alexander Kuznetsov, the 1st Assault Detachment drove straight into Rostov, secured parts of the city and the peacetime headquarters of OSK South. Around 06.00hrs local time, Prigozhin appeared in Rostov to meet the Deputy Defence Minister Yunus-Bek Yevkurov and several other top officers. In a video taken during that meeting, he explained that his forces had shot down several VKS helicopters 'shooting at civilians', but that he had no intention of interfering with the work of OSK South against Ukraine. He 'merely' demanded to talk to the 'Chief-of-Staff' (Gerasimov), and accused Yevkurov of pushing thousands of troops to their deaths, without ammunition and or a plan.

During Prigozhin's meeting with Yevkurov, additional assault detachments reached Rostov: following careful coordination between their commanders, at least two of these continued their journey further west and south: one secured Taganrog AB, while the other advanced on Krasnodar, to the south. Just like the advance on Moscow, around 18.00hrs, their further operations were stopped following intervention by the Belarussian president Lukashenko.

Alexander 'Ratibor' Kuznetsov, commander of the 1st Assault Detachment as of the first half of 2023 and during the mutiny in June of that year. (Russian social media)

Unlike its practices from Libya and Syria, in Ukraine, the Wagner Group was initially deployed primarily in roles for which other nations might deploy their special forces assets. Correspondingly, it was only during the reorganisations of the late summer and autumn of 2022 that the mercenaries began operating heavier weapons to bolster the firepower of their assault detachments. Henceforth, many of these resembled the organisation and equipment of the different 'Liwa(s)' organised, equipped and trained by the Islamic Revolutionary Guards Corps during the wars in Iraq and Syria during the previous decade. Unsurprisingly, Wagner was quick to create numerous 'technicals': usually light trucks like this GAZ-66, which received armour plating around its cab and cargo hold, and a twin-barrel 23mm ZU-23 autocannon. (Artwork by David Bocquelet)

Amongst the first pieces of 'regular' heavy equipment noted as operated by the Wagner Group were examples such this BMD-3 light infantry fighting vehicle sighted in September 2022. Developed in the 1980s and with the first examples delivered in 1990, few were built due to the economic situation in the USSR and Russia at that time. Their original purpose was to provide the VDV with a fully amphibious and air-droppable (with the crew of three inside) vehicle carrying a stabilised 30mm 2A42 autocannon (with 500 rounds), and a 9P135M missile launcher for 9K111 Fagot and 9M113 Konkurs anti-tank guided missiles. It offered space for seven dismounts. This armament configuration proved its worth in combat in Ukraine, although the amour made of aluminium alloy proved much too easy to penetrate even by 7.62mm machine guns, not to mention heavier weapons. (Artwork by David Bocquelet)

With the reorganisation of its BTGs into assault detachments in late summer and autumn of 2022, the Wagner Group began introducing to service a growing number of BMP-2 infantry fighting vehicles. Their principal armament was the same as that of the BMD-3, but their armour proved of much better quality. Typically, one BMP-2 (or BMD-3) was assigned to each assault group, together with a single main battle tank, two mortars (82mm or 120mm), one AGS-17 automatic grenade launcher, and one D-30 howitzer. This BMP-2, largely covered by camouflage netting, belonged to an unidentified assault detachment involved in the advance from Voronezh towards Moscow on 24 June 2024. (Artwork by David Bocquelet)

As in Africa, the Wagner Group deployed numerous Ural-432007 Chekan (shown here) and Shchuka MRAPs in Ukraine. However, the type rapidly proved too thin-skinned for operations in high-threat areas and was usually relegated to secondary tasks; often even retro-converted into trucks with a (thinly) armoured cab. This is a reconstruction of a Chekan still in its original configuration, based upon a vehicle found shot-up and abandoned in the Bakhmut area in March 2023. (Artwork by David Bocquelet)

One new type of vehicle introduced to service by the Wagner Group in late 2022 was the Moscow Military Industrial Company 'Spartak' armoured car. Developed in the late 2010s, it entered service in 2021–2022. This vehicle is about 6.5m long, 2.8m tall, and weighs 14.5 tons. It has a welded armoured hull offering protection from up to 12.7–14.5mm projectiles, with space for the crew of two and eight passengers. This is a reconstruction of an example seen in service with Wagner in Rostov on 24 June 2023. (Artwork by David Bocquelet)

During 2023, with help from the Ministry of Defence in Moscow, the Wagner Group began replacing its 'do-it-yourself' armoured vehicles with better types, including BTR-82As, one of which is shown here. A further development of the BTR-80 and -80A (in turn improved from the older and relatively unsuccessful BTR-70 armoured personnel carrier), this 8-wheeled vehicle first seen in the mid-1990s received a new single engine, improved armour, spall liners, a GLONASS navigation system and a turret with the 30mm 2A72 autocannon and TKN-4GA-02 night-vision device. The Wagner Group also received a few 2S23 Nona-SVK self-propelled 120mm mortars mounted on the same chassis, and both remained in service and were seen in numbers during the mutiny of 24 June 2023. (Artwork by David Bocquelet)

In April 2023, during the Battle of Bakhmut, the Wagner Group captured a number of ZSU-operated armoured vehicles. One for which there is enough visual evidence available to enable a reconstruction was this M113A3. Such vehicles were donated to Ukraine from the surplus stocks of several countries including Australia, Denmark, Germany, Portugal, Spain, and the USA. The vehicle's dark green overall livery was massively weathered and dirty: the mercenaries then added a large white 'Z' as a means of quick visual identification. As far as is known, this M113 had no armament while in Russian service, indicating that it was probably used for transport purposes only. (Artwork by David Bocquelet)

Since its tour in Libya during 2018–2019, the principal air defence system of the Wagner Group was the Pantsir S2. The system included a total of 12 ready-to-fire 95YA6-2/2M missiles and two dual 30mm 2A38M autocannons. Unlike the version developed for the UAE and mounted on a German-made MAN SX 45 8x8 truck (see Volume 1), the version usually operated in Ukraine was mounted on the Russian-made KAMAZ-6560 38 ton, 400hp (300kW), truck. As far as is known, all the Wagner-operated Pantsirs in Ukraine were painted in olive green overall: most had a large white 'Z' on their cabin and superstructure, usually applied crudely by hand and brush. (Artwork by Anderson Subtil)

During the reorganisation in the late summer and autumn of 2022, the Wagner Group began receiving advanced variants of the T-72 family of main battle tanks. Most of these were T-72Bs, upgraded through adding ever-larger amounts of *Kontakt*-5 ERA around the turret, and additional steel containers on the glacis and side skirts. Indeed, examples like this T-72B3M received the new *Relikt* ERA, laser detectors of the *Shtora* complex, the A246M-5 gun with a modified autoloader (making them compatible with ammunition for the T-90A), the *Sosna*-U integrated gunner's thermal sight and fire control system, an improved radio, and the V-92S2 engine. This vehicle was last seen in the Voronezh area, on 24 June 2023. (Artwork by David Bocquelet)

In late 2022, mercenaries of the Wagner Group began publicly bragging of the acquisition of the latest T-90 main battle tanks. Amongst these were several T-90Ss drawn from a shipment of vehicles owned by India and sent to Russia for upgrade, or from the stock of demonstration vehicles. Primary armament of these vehicles was the 2A46M-2 smoothbore 125mm gun with an autoloader (and an ammunition capacity of 42 rounds). Secondary armament included a Kord 12.7mm heavy machine gun on the *Utyos* remotely-controlled mount), and a coaxially installed PKMT 7.62mm machine gun. Following the mutiny of June 2023, all were reappropriated by the VSRF. (Artwork by David Bocquelet)

Except for the Pantsir S2, probably the most advanced fighting vehicle operated by the Wagner Group was a handful of T-90M main battle tanks (also known as '*Proryv*-3' or simply '*Proryv*', meaning 'Breakthrough'). Based on the T-72, and in service only since 2020, these received *Relikt* ERA, a new, modular turret with a stretched bustle (containing 10 rounds for the main gun), the *Kalina* fire control system (an upgraded version of the *Sosna*-U), and the T105BV-1 remote-controlled machine gun mount with, in the case of the vehicle shown here, a PKTM 7.62mm machine gun. The Wagner mercenaries found the vehicle superior to any of the earlier Russian tanks, but also lacking in terms of cross-country mobility due to their additional armour and equipment. (Artwork by David Bocquelet)

In addition to more modern T-72B3s and various marks of T-90s, the Wagner Group also operated a number of T-80s. Once widely considered a 'premium' tank reserved for elite formations, and certainly more expensive to manufacture and with a high level of fuel consumption, by 2022 most of those still in service with the VSRF had been upgraded to the T-80BVM variant, which included the installation of the modernised 2A46M-4 gun, *Relikt* ERA and the *Sosna*-U- or even the 1PN-96MT thermal sight. Nicknamed *Sibir* (*Siberia*), this non-upgraded T-80BV, originally manufactured in the mid-1980s, survived long enough to receive the red 'V' and the 'Z' markings applied to some mercenary-operated vehicles during the mutiny of 23–24 June 2023. (Artwork by David Bocquelet)

Above left: Almost right from the start of its involvement in Putin's all-out invasion of Ukraine in 2022 the Wagner Group began recruiting in Africa and the Middle East. As a result, numerous nationals from the Central African Republic, Iraq, Libya, Mali, and Syria ended up fighting within its ranks. This Palestinian volunteer (almost certainly recruited in Syria) is shown wearing the Guerrilla Panacea EMR uniform (usually issued to the Spetsnaz), with oversized winter boots made of black leather. His firearm is an AK-74M. (Artwork by Giorgio Albertini)

Above right: A typical Russian mercenary serving with the Wagner Group in the Bakhmut area in 2022–2023, wearing Jastreb helmet with cover (often completed with a GSSh-01 communication set), multicam pattern autumn jacket, Sumrak Bars M2 pattern trousers, and black Faraday 443 boots. Shown on his chest are the Flora EMR pattern body armour and so-called 'fast reload ammo pouches' (frequently completed by RGN or RGO pouches for hand-grenades, usually carried on the back). His firearm is an AK-12 rifle – here shown without the frequently-used PKU-2 scope or AK-2 Noch flash suppressor. (Artwork by Giorgio Albertini)

Left: A few mercenaries from Serbia had served with the Wagner Group in Syria since 2015: about 150 were contracted for deployment to Ukraine from early 2023. Their camouflage fatigues were drawn from a wide variety of sources, with some even wearing uniforms of the Russian Ministry of Internal Affairs. Most were issued with Jastreb helmets, shown here with 6B34 Permyachka goggles in their protective cover, and AK-74/74Ms. (Artwork by Giorgio Albertini)

With grudging permission from the Ministry of Defence in Moscow, the Wagner Group began contracting veteran fighter pilots of the VKS for service in Africa in 2017–2018, and by 2019 its crews also served in Libya. In summer 2022, enough mercenaries were grouped together to man a squadron of Sukhoi Su-25s in each of the 18th Assault and the 255th Attack Aviation regiments. Operating from Buturlinovka, Kursk-Vostochny, and Millerovo ABs in Russia, mercenary-operated jets like the one shown here (overhauled and repainted but not upgraded to Su-25SM standard) thus became heavily involved in the fighting for Popasna and Bakhmut. Bort 15 is shown armed with B-8M pods for 80mm unguided rockets. (Artwork by Tom Cooper)

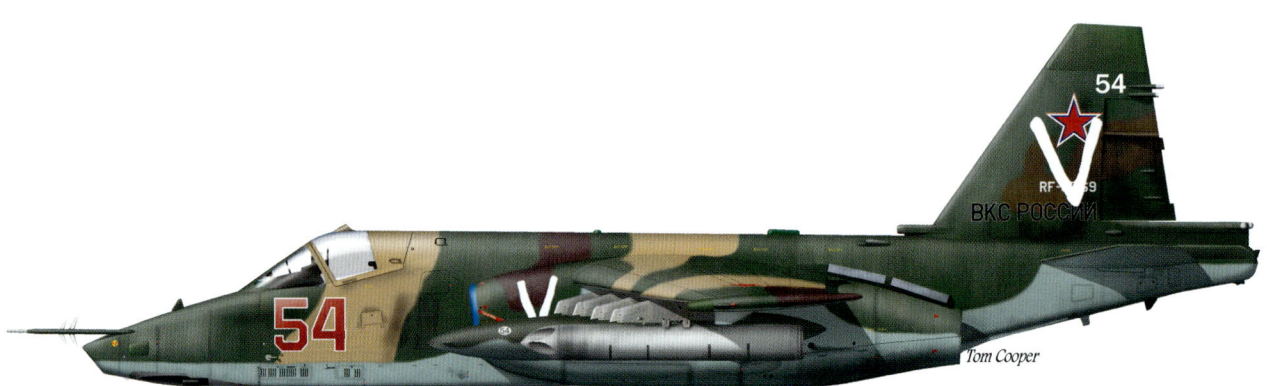

While their heavy losses early during the invasion prompted VKS units to avoid operating directly over the battlefield, mercenary fliers continued doing so and frequently flew repeated air strikes employing 80mm and 130mm unguided rockets and free-fall bombs. While a number of jets flown by Wagner pilots were damaged, they are known to have suffered only two resulting losses, including Colonel Nikolai Markov, killed on 30 April, and Major General Kanamat Huseinovich Botashev, killed on 22 May. This Su-25SM from the 18th Assault Aviation Regiment is shown as it appeared in early 2023. Unlike the example shown at the top of this page it retained its registration (RF-95169), while having large white V markings on the intake and fin as a method of quick visual identification. (Artwork by Tom Cooper)

By autumn 2022, the Wager Group was also staffing an entire squadron operating Sukhoi Su-24M fighter-bombers of an unknown regiment of the VKS. Unlike the Su-25s, these were primarily equipped with bombs: usually FAB-250M-62s (shown under the inboard underwing pylon) and FAB-500M-62s. Alternative armament consisted of up to four MBD3-U6-68 racks, each with four to six 50kg OFAB-50 or 100kg OFAB-100 bombs. Some witnesses to their attacks compared the effects to barrages from BM-21 multiple rocket launchers. This Su-24M (Bort 48, registration RF-93798) was shot down while trying to attack a ZSU unit involved in the fighting for Klishchivka, south of Bakhmut, on 2 December 2022. The crew, consisting of Lieutenant Colonel (ret.) Alexander Sergeyevich Antonov and Major (ret.) Vladimir Nikolaevich Nikishin, was killed. (Artwork by Tom Cooper)

In addition to Su-24s and Su-25s, veteran VKS personnel recruited by Wagner and serving in Ukraine also manned at least a small squadron equipped with several variants of the Mil Mi-8 helicopter. Amongst these were such relatively modern examples as this Mi-8AMTSh, which belonged to a subvariant with the classic rear cabin shape, but without the large clamshell doors removed for easier disembarkation (as in widespread service with the VKS during 2022–2023; see *War in Ukraine Volume 6* for details). Moreover, it had only part of the L370E8 Vitebsk self-protection suite: a single L370-2 UV missile approach warning sensor under the left side of the cockpit. Bort 42 is shown armed with B-8B pods for 80mm S-8 unguided rockets. (Artwork by Tom Cooper)

The history of the Wagner Group's involvement in the War in Ukraine was full of ironies. One of these was that its assaults on Popasna and Bakhmut were heavily supported by Kamov Ka-52 attack helicopters: indeed, these flew hundreds of attacks on Ukrainian positions that were assaulted by the mercenaries. However, during the mutiny of 24 June 2023, at least one of the Wagner columns marching in the direction of Moscow came under attack by Ka-52s. In turn, Bort 72 (registration RF-13418) from the 15th Army Aviation Brigade was shot down by either Pantsir S2 or Strela-10 air defence systems operated by the Wagner Group. Its crew, consisting of Lieutenant Colonel Alexei Vorozhtsov and Lieutenant Denis Oleinikov, was killed when their helicopter crashed outside the village of Komintern in the Talovsky Raion of Voronezh Oblast. (Artwork by Luca Canossa)

Another irony of 24 June 2023 was that during their march through Voronezh Oblast, the Wagner mercenaries opened fire at an aircraft that had certainly played an important role during their earlier operations in Ukraine: this Ilyushin Il-22M-11 airborne command post (registration RA-75917) of the 610th Centre of Combat Application and Retraining (headquartered at Ivanovo AB). The aircraft crashed near Kantemirovka, killing all eight crew members, consisting of Lieutenant Colonel Artem Milovanov, Major Gennady Belyakin, captains Artem Sharoglazov, Igor Volochilov, and Viktor Popov, and senior sergeants Alexey Skrykov Sergey Starushok, and Viktor Podrepny. (Artwork by Tom Cooper)

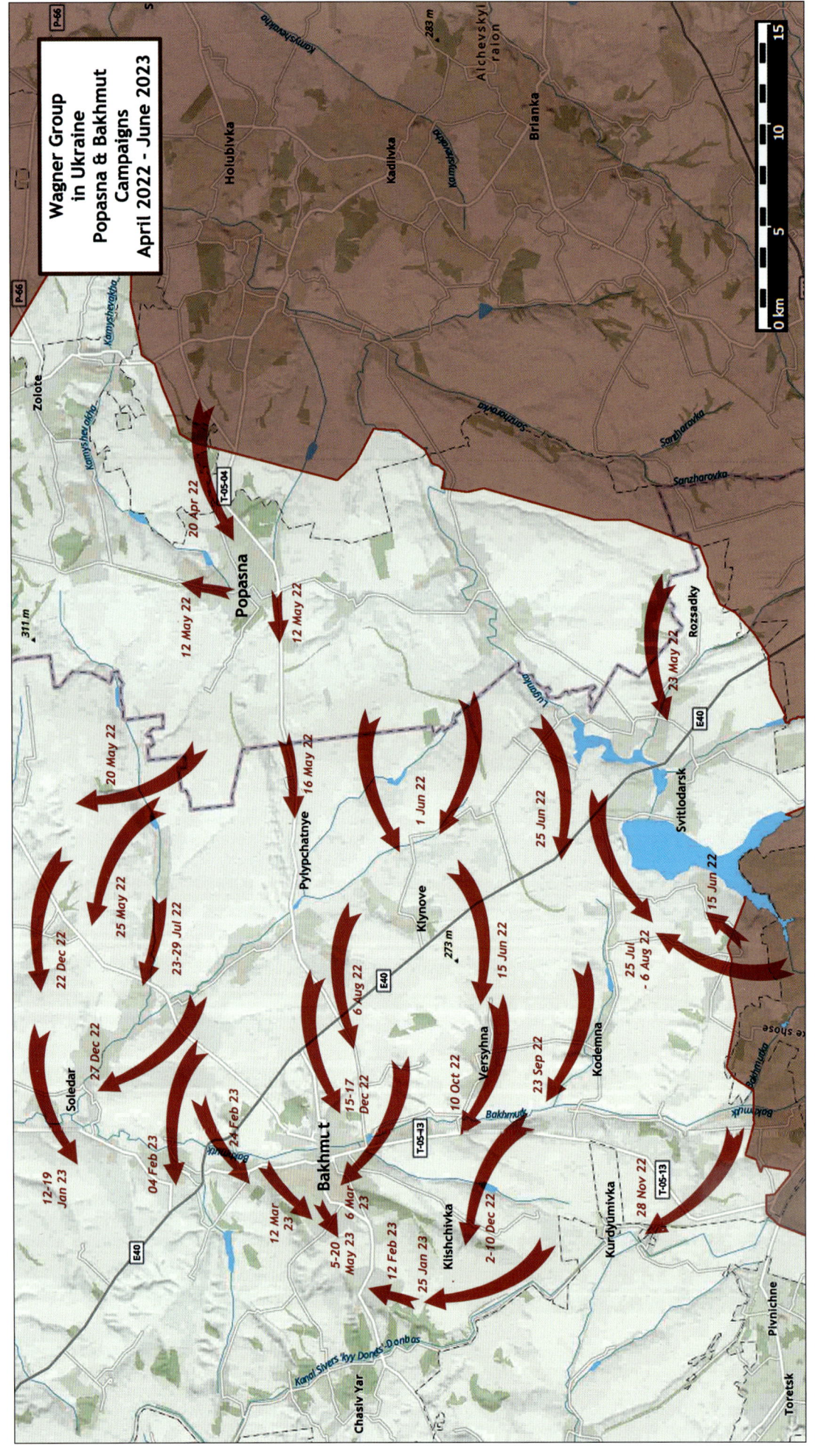

The Wagner Group's campaigns in the Popasna and Bakhmut areas from April 2022 until June 2023. (Map by Tom Cooper)

Above: A Pantsir S1 truck-mounted short-range air defence system of the Wagner Group navigating its way through the morning traffic outside Rostov. (Russian social media)

Right: Burning wreckage of one of four helicopters shot down by Wagner mercenaries during clashes north-east of Rostov-na-Donu early on 24 June 2023. (Russian social media)

Below: Wagner mercenaries outside the headquarters of OSK South, in Rostov-na-Donu, early on 24 June 2022. (TASS)

Reactions

Numerous experts around the world were astonished by the fact that Wagner faced no armed resistance at all from the military, border guards, or police, even though Putin made it clear in his Address to citizens of Russia on the morning of 24 June 2023 that the coup was 'a knife in the back of our country and our people', a 'criminal adventure', a 'betrayal', an 'armed mutiny' on the path of 'blackmail and terrorism' and that the Russian military and government agencies had 'received the necessary orders'.[19]

Russian Army General Sergey Surovikin ('General Armageddon),[20] and Lieutenant General Alexeyev, First Deputy Chief of the Main Directorate of the General Staff of the Armed Forces of the Russian Federation, issued statements on 24 June 2023 concerning the armed mutiny, demanding that Prigozhin and his troops must avoid bloodshed, stop the mutiny and comply with Putin's orders.[21] The two generals were sent to negotiate with Prigozhin at the Headquarters of the Southern Military District in Rostov-on-Don,[22] occupied at that time by Wagner troops. However, Prigozhin rejected the demands and the offers of the two generals.[23]

Without anyone informing the Russian public, Belarusian President Lukashenko negotiated 'all day' on 24 June 2023 with Prigozhin in order to reach a deal to avoid a bloodbath. Lukashenko acted based on the mandate that he had from Putin. On the afternoon of 24 June 2023, a deal was reached that resulted in a drastic turning point for the armed coup. Russian mainstream media, referring to the announcements of Lukashenko's official state media, made public some key points of the deal between Lukashenko and Prigozhin. These key issues are the following:

- The organization of a bloodbath on the territory of Russia was entirely unacceptable.
- Prigozhin must stop the advance of his troops on Russian territory.
- Prigozhin and Wagner's 'employees' receive a security guarantee: they would not be prosecuted by the Russian state and criminal charges would be dropped, with 'Putin's word' as a guarantee for this.

None of this had been confirmed by the Russian president, the Russian Ministry of Foreign Affairs, or anyone else, when the negotiations between Lukashenko and Prigozhin took place. Official confirmation followed later on. Although precise details remain unclear, the deal between Lukashenko and Prigozhin deserves analysis.

Lukashenko must have told Prigozhin that he and his team, but also their family members were certain to be killed should the mercenaries enter the centre of Moscow. The key Russian forces foremost the 14,000-strong Derzhinsky Special Forces Division of the Rosgvardia, responsible directly to Putin – prepared their positions to fight Wagner to the death, if necessary, in the heavily populated urban environment of Moscow. The Russian defence line should not be confused with the outskirts of Moscow, a circle consisting of a relatively loosely built, more-or-less village-like environment, stretching for tens of kilometres from the centre, where no serious defences were built, if any.

Prigozhin was strong when operating with Russian air superiority, artillery superiority, supply of weapons and ammunition against the Ukrainian Armed Forces. But the Wagner Group as a force of armed mutiny against the top military leadership in Moscow was weak on its own, on Russian territory, and against the Russian state.

Knowing the content of Putin's second speech following the suppression of Prigozhin's armed mutiny, on 24 June 2023, it became clear, that not only were decisions made to suppress the armed mutiny, but also decisions were made to avoid spilling blood.[24] Correspondingly, the Rosgvardia and other units possibly in the way of Wagner's march to Moscow received orders not to engage in armed resistance to the Wagner mutiny. Russian units possessing nuclear weapons were most likely exceptions to such an order, since if Prigozhin gained control of nuclear strike capabilities, it could have been an utmost stressful nightmare scenario. Should such an event have occured, even though Prigozhin's Wagner did not have the 'know how' to operate the Russian nuclear arsenal, Prigozhin had the theoretical possibility to obtain the 'know how' from captured and interrogated key Russian military personnel. Such a scenario had to be avoided by Moscow at all costs. The authors doubt that there were safety features 'built in' to the Russian nuclear strike capabilities that were 'by definition' impossible for Wagner to overcome by use of extreme methods of interrogating local personnel.

Putin's second speech during Wagner's armed mutiny on 24 June 2023 made it clear that efforts had been made by Moscow to avoid bloodshed. This fact makes understandable, what seemed astonishing until then, that the Wagner Group had not encountered Russian armed resistance on the ground, even when getting close to Moscow. The reason was that Moscow was waiting for the outcome of the negotiations between Lukashenko and Prigozhin to make the final decision whether the bloodshed was going to be inevitable or not.

When talking about lack of armed resistance by the Russian military during the Wagner armed mutiny this does not mean that the Russian military did not resist Wagner by non-lethal methods. The three downed Russian electronic warfare helicopters, being 'unarmed', described by Russian media as 'completely innocent' since they were allegedly performing planned duties independent of the mutiny, could have possibly been used by Moscow to suppress Wagner's communications, air defences and other electronic activity. The authors are inclined to believe the active, but non-lethal suppression version of events, rather than the 'innocent' version claimed by Moscow. This judgement is purely based on the logic of how the world's militaries operate.

It was later revealed that the widely reported shooting in Rostov was not a firefight, but rather Russian soldiers firing into the air to disperse civilians. Ultimately, Prigozhin, like most Wagner fighters, did not wish to die. Nevertheless, he was directly responsible for the downing of six Russian military helicopters and two aircraft. The prosecution of Prigozhin and his private military company was ultimately abandoned when criminal charges were officially dropped against him and all Wagner Group members.

The Wagner Group's military capabilities and effectiveness have consistently drawn attention, whether judged positively or negatively, when analysing various historical periods and the diverse operations they undertook. During the armed mutiny aimed at removing Russia's top military leadership, Wagner's performance in some respects surpassed that of the Ukrainian state. While their advance was limited to narrow zones and did not involve holding hundreds of kilometres of front lines, it demonstrated significant tactical effectiveness.

Meanwhile, Russian mainstream media claimed that during the first three weeks of Ukraine's heavily promoted counteroffensive in the summer of 2023 – an operation intended not only to reclaim substantial territory from Russian control but also to sever the land connection between Crimea and mainland Russia – the Ukrainian Armed Forces failed to down a single Russian military helicopter.

One might suggest that Russian military losses against their own troops, such as Wagner, on Russian territory are incomparable to those along the Russian-Ukrainian front line. There is much truth is such an argument, since the majority of the Russian military activity against Wagner excluded any lethal damage. On the other hand, the Russian military leadership took some unusually high risks to gather information about the armed mutiny, since there was hope that Wagner would not down the aircraft involved. While probably related to 'routine' operations against Ukraine, the use of the Il-22 aircraft was a good example – as such a valuable aircraft would never be operated within reach of the ZSU.

It also deserves an in-depth analysis, whether Wagner's failed coup was an 'armed mutiny' or really a 'march of equity', as claimed by Prigorzhin. The short answer is that it was an armed mutiny, since it was not agreed with the Kremlin, its aim was to remove the top Russian military leadership, and that hundreds of tanks and other military vehicles marching to conquer the Russian capital, initially fully rejecting the offers of the Russian Ministry of Defence, would inevitably meet all legal arguments to call it an armed mutiny, and nothing else – precisely as branded by Putin. However, the next sub-chapter will provide much more detailed evidence than what has been analysed thus far, proving that no serious analysis might support the idea that Prigozhin did not intend to make an armed mutiny, but rather a kind of a 'benevolent' chain of actions, a 'march of equity'.

Prigozhin's Story

During Prigozhin's first public appearance following the failed armed mutiny, he attempted to prevent being discredited 'beyond repair'.

> According to Prigozhin, on 30 June, the PMC convoy was going to head to Rostov-on-Don and publicly transfer military equipment near the headquarters of the Southern Eastern District. The Wagner founder repeated his statement that the PMC units had allegedly been hit by a missile attack, as a result of which the fighters decided to advance ahead of schedule. The Ministry of Defence called the information about the shelling of the positions of the "Wagnerites" an "information provocation." During the march, one column advanced to Rostov, the other to Moscow, Prigozhin said. According to him, in a day they covered 780 km, blocking military units, airfields and other military facilities that were along the way.[25]

No evidence was presented by Prigozhin or in Russian media, proving the allegations of the Wagner chief concerning Russian bombardment of his troops.

Prigozhin's story suggesting an early handover of heavy military equipment to Russia, that was originally planned to be done on 30 June 2023, as quoted previously, does not withstand any serious analysis. Handing over military equipment requires agreement between the parties involved: in this case, between Prigozhin's Wagner and the Russian Ministry of Defence. Equipment should not be transported to the Headquarters of the Southern Military District, but to the base(es) detailed in the agreement. Heavy military equipment should not reach the destination on tracks, but on trailers to avoid damaging the roads. Military convoys should always be escorted by police and/or military police. And ultimately, the handover of heavy military equipment did not take place at all when the armed mutiny failed and the Wagner Group's columns left Russia.

Similar misinformation on the part of Prigozhin and some analysts siding with him claims that by not showing armed resistance against the Wagner Group columns, the Russian Ministry of Defence proved its total defencelessness, unprofessionalism, and weakness:

> it became clear that the Russian "elite" was completely unprepared not only to save their country during the war, but could easily escape from it … And if it weren't for the Wagner PMC, but for the Ukrainian division? Regiment

Prigozhin (centre) in negotiations with the Deputy Defence Minister of the Russian Federation, Yunus-Bek Yevkurov (left), in Rostov-na-Donu, early on 24 June 2023. (Wagner PMC)

of paratroopers thrown out near Rostov? Would the armed forces of the Russian Federation be ready to repel the blow competently and without panic? Unfortunately, the breakthroughs of enemy reconnaissance and diversion units in the Bryansk region indicate the opposite … So Prigozhin's "march" showed how the innocent are rewarded and the innocent are punished…[26]

It was a typical distortion of information. Should a Russian political decision have not been made at the very beginning of the armed mutiny by President Putin, ordering not to shoot at the Wagner columns, fighting and a bloodbath would have started as soon as the first column of Prigozhin's soldiers attempted to cross the Russian border. Should the Russian top leadership had decided to suppress the armed mutiny of Prigozhin by military force, rather than negotiations avoiding bloodshed, the Russian Ministry of Defence would have had plenty of opportunities to show armed resistance. Russian Aerospace Forces could have been put on alert and ordered to bombard the military columns of Wagner. Minefields could have been planted by Russian aircraft on the roads and in their vicinity, where Wagner's columns were expected to push forward. Russian special forces could have received orders to occupy defensive positions to halt Wagner. It is utterly unfair to claim that no armed resistance against Wagner's columns at the beginning of the armed mutiny equated to a total impotence and incompetence of the Russian state. Since Prigozhin and his supporters used such arguments against the Russian state and the top military leadership, they discredited themselves in the eyes of those who are capable of a critical analysis of what happened.

Prigozhin was playing a dangerous and irresponsible game when suggesting that 'he is against conditional traitors within the system, who by their actions and inaction caused more damage than the enemy.'[27]

We need to keep in mind that Russian citizens who provide false information thereby discrediting the Russian Armed Forces capabilities, actions, etc., could be subjected to criminal investigation and punishment in Russia.

Prigozhin's last Meeting with Putin

On 29 June 2023, a meeting took place in the Kremlin between Prigozhin, with 35 of his field commanders and other representatives of Wagner, and Putin. Since the meeting lasted for three hours, all important members of Wagner had a chance to express their opinions, and Putin addressed all opinions, clarifying his own position. The parties:

"emphasized that they are staunch supporters and soldiers of the head of state and the Supreme Commander-in-Chief, and also said that they were ready to continue to fight for the Motherland." It is clear from Peskov's words that Putin handled the situation well, confirming the legitimacy of the Wagner fighters, but insisting on defining their actions as a "mutiny." … the finances of PMC "Wagner" will be significantly cut. This will happen due to the conclusion of contracts for the nutrition of the Ministry of Defence with another firm or firms.[28]

According to analysts, Prigozhin had three major demands:

1. sacking Russian Defence Minister, General of the Army, Sergey Shoygu,
2. sacking of Russian Chief of Staff, General of the Army, Valery Gerasimov,
3. to have a personal meeting with Russian president, Vladimir Putin.[29]

The third demand had been fulfilled, the first two were subjects of speculation. In the following months it would be a fact of history, whether the demands of Prigozhin concerning the sacking of the top Russian military leadership would come true or not.

Financing Scheme of the Wagner Group

Subsequently, Putin has disclosed previously unknown details concerning Russian state's sponsorship of the Wagner Group. It had been known that the Russian state paid huge, secret sums of money to Wagner, especially to support their military activities in Ukraine, but the extent of official financing was unavailable in open source documents.[30] Putin claimed that Wagner had been fully paid by the Russian state, naming annual sums:[31]

I would like to point out, and I want everyone to be aware of the fact that all of the funding the Wagner Group received came from the state. It got all its funding from us, from the Defence Ministry, from the state budget. Between May 2022 and May 2023 alone, the Wagner Group received 86,262 million rubles [approximately 0.89 billion USD][32] from the state to pay military salaries and bonuses, including 70,384 million rubles [approximately 0.72 billion USD] for payroll and 15,877 million rubles [approximately 0.16 billion USD] for paying out bonuses. Insurance premiums totalled 110,179 million [approximately 1.13 billion USD]. But while the state

Funeral for the 10 crew-members of the Il-22M-11 aircraft shot down by Wagner's mercenaries on 24 June. (Russian social media)

covered all of the Wagner Group's funding needs, the company's owner, Concord, received from the state, or should I say earned, 80 billion rubles [approximately 0.82 billion USD] through Voentorg as the army's food and canteen provider. The state covered all its funding needs, while part of the group – I mean Concord – made 80 billion rubles, all at the same time.³³

Putin's claims concerning the financing scheme of the Wagner are in sharp contradiction of that of Prigozhin, who claimed entirely the opposite, suggesting that he spent his own money on financing Wagner and he served Russian interests worldwide for free, while insisting, that the Wagner Group was not even a PMC – even when this abbreviation was widely used in memorabilia of his mercenaries:

> We have never been a PMC. And we have never made profit as a private military company. We participated in various conflicts, defending the interests of the Russian Federation, in some cases, protecting the local population as well. In 99% of cases, we did it absolutely free. I spent about one and a half billion dollars of my own money, according to estimates at the beginning of the Special Military Operation … According to the head of the Wagnerites, the only contract that was supposed to make a profit was a contract to liberate oil fields in the Syrian Republic in 2016. We agreed with Assad that we would receive twenty percent of the sales of oil, which we would win back for them.³⁴

Since the failed armed mutiny of the Wagner Group a lot of interest appeared worldwide, especially in Russia, to have at least a summary of what amount of money the Russian PMC received from the Russian state since its establishment. While Putin detailed only the yearly income of the Wagner Group, mainstream Russian media 'served' the data many were eager to know. Dmitry Kiselev, a leading television host on the *Russia 1 (Россия 1)* TV channel provided his data referring to his information sources:

> The private military company Wagner founded by Yevgeny Prigozhin, received a little more than 858 billion roubles under contracts concluded with the state. This is about a trillion. Under other contracts, Prigozhin's holding Concorde provided services in the amount of 845 billion roubles. This

One much-overlooked aspect of the Wagner Group was the foreign mercenaries serving with the PMC. This video still shows two from Mali and a Palestinian in early 2023. (Russian social media)

does not mean that the PMC actually earned that much money, but [as it was contracted] it still speaks of the scale of the business and the scale of ambitions, Kiselev said.³⁵

Wagner Group's Military Equipment

It is difficult to get a realistic picture of Wagner military equipment in Ukraine due to lack of reliable open source information.³⁶ However, some Russian sources have provided detailed information concerning military equipment used in the armed mutiny on 24–25 June 2023.³⁷

> The first column, in which there were about 350 pieces of equipment, crossed the border of the Voronezh region immediately after midnight on June 24. There were nine tanks, four Tigers, Grad MLRS', a howitzer, dozens of trucks and hundreds of cars in the column. It was this column that later demolished a barrier of trucks and construction equipment … At about 05.00 a.m., a second convoy drove into the region,

A group of Serbian mercenaries serving with the Wagner Group, seen here in January 2023. Nearly 200 Serbian nationals have served with this PMC since 2015, initially in Syria, and – especially since early 2023 – in Ukraine, where they were officially assigned to the 15th 'Pyatnashka' or 'International' Motor-Rifle Brigade, subordinated to the Wagner Group. (Serbian social media)

even more – approximately 375 pieces of equipment, it moved towards the city of Buturlinovka – to a military airfield. At 07.00, the third convoy drove into the Voronezh region, in which there were about 100 pieces of equipment: three tanks, two anti-aircraft guns, buses, trucks and cars. The column went along the M-4 "Don" highway. At 09.00, the fourth column crossed the border of the region – 212 units.[38]

In total, there were approximately 1,137 pieces of equipment in these four major columns alone, most of which consisted of armoured vehicles, trucks, and cars. This provides some insight into the scale of Wagner's resources in Ukraine, though it is likely that not all personnel or equipment was involved in the armed mutiny. Additionally, some Russian sources, citing information from the Russian Ministry of Defence, reported that Wagner was required to hand over its 'heavy' military equipment to the Russian Army.[39] It remains unclear what exactly was meant by this. However, the issue is now largely irrelevant, not only because Wagner was required to surrender all types of military equipment to the Russian Ministry of Defence – including small arms, light weapons, and thousands of tons of ammunition – but also because the group was disbanded and its successors reorganised. The scale of the weapon confiscation was a political decision, approved by Putin. It is still uncertain whether the confiscation affected only Wagner's Ukrainian contingent, which participated in the mutiny, or the entire organization, including its operations and equipment in Africa and Latin America.

This was a very significant change not only affecting the military capabilities of the Wagner Group but also showing a major shift of the concept how the Russian state wanted to use it in the future. Since Wagner lost most of its military equipment in favour of the Russian state, it would be unable to perform significant offensive or defensive operations without the cooperation and assistance of the Russian Armed Forces. Furthermore, it would be unable to stage a significant armed mutiny as it did on 23-24 June 2023. This is a very important issue since no serious leadership of any country would want to be threatened after a successful suppression of an armed mutiny. The fact that the Rosgvardia subsequently began to receive heavy equipment, that it did not have before,[40] proves, that the top Russian leadership understands the key importance of having heavy weaponry when suppressing an armed mutiny, and that it also makes a big difference, whether the rebel leadership possesses heavy weaponry or not.

Even more became known about Wagner's military equipment on 12 July 2023, when the Russian Ministry of Defence published a report on the final stage of Wagner handing over all forms of military equipment (and not just the heavy equipment):[41]

Including hundreds of heavy weapons: T-90, T-80, T-72B3 tanks, Grad and Uragan multiple launch rocket systems, Pantsir anti-aircraft missile and gun systems, 122-mm 2S1 Gvozdika self-propelled artillery mounts, 152-mm 2S3 Akatsiya, 152-mm 2S5 Hyacinth, 240-mm 2S4 Tulip, howitzers and anti-tank guns, mortar systems, multi-purpose armoured tractors, armoured personnel carriers, as well as vehicles and small arms. Among the transferred equipment, dozens of units have never been used in combat conditions. More than two and a half thousand tons of various ammunition and about 20,000 small arms have also been received [by the Russian Ministry of Defence from the Wagner Group]. Heavy tracked vehicles, high-capacity self-propelled artillery mounts and tanks are brought to field bases by wheeled tractors on trailers in order to prevent damage to asphalt roads. Wheeled vehicles arrive on their own. All equipment and weapons are delivered to the rear areas, where the repair and restoration units of the Armed Forces of the Russian Federation carry out maintenance and preparation for their intended use.[42]

A BMP-2 infantry fighting vehicle loaded on a civilian trailer is seen here on the M-4 Highway during the advance on Moscow on 24 June 2023. (Russian social media)

Above: The rear of a BTR-82A wheeled armoured personnel carrier of the Wagner Group on the eastern approaches to Bakhmut, as seen on 29 May 2023. (via Dean O'Brien)

Left: A Pantsir S1 air defence system, operated by the Wagner Group, seen during the mutiny of June 2023. (Russian social media)

Short-lived Exile in Belarus

According to Belarusian President Lukashenko, following their mutiny, the pardoned commanders of the Wagner PMC were to transfer their war experience to the Belorussian Armed Forces, especially concerning the stormtroopers' experience on the front line.[43] They were to share their experiences with weapons, too: which worked well, which did not: "…and tactics, and weapons, and how to attack, how to defend. It's priceless. This is what we need to take from the Wagnerites."[44]

Some Russian sources claimed that there would be two Wagner military bases in Belarus, each accommodating 8,500 people, the financing of which was already agreed.[45] It is not clear whether the Russian state, the Belarussian state, or both were to finance the above-mentioned bases, but it was clear that they would not be financed by Prigozhin. There was to be a third Wagner base in Belarus, able to accommodate 12,000–15,000 people. This would be a training base financed by Prigozhin, utilising his business income from Africa.[46] However, other Russian sources claimed, citing Lukashenko, that no Wagner bases were built in Belarus and there was no recruitment of Wagner soldiers. Should Wagner soldiers want accommodation in Belarus, they were free to get it.[47] Since other sources even claimed that they possessed satellite pictures of the alleged Wagner bases being built, it might be assumed that they were more credible than those who simply denied that Wagner bases were being built in Belarus. President Lukashenko's official position was difficult to deny on the other hand, since he acknowledged that Wagner soldiers could have accommodation in Belarus. Of course, this could have been civilian flats rented or purchased by Wagner military personnel, but common accommodation with Belorussian troops seemed to be even more evident. It all appeared to be 'fog of war' and sooner or later more information will surely appear on this topic. The Wagner bases in Crimea would remain there, and training and recruiting continued. Utkin, one of the key figures of Wagner, would travel to Belarus, the most likely reason being his military expertise, including war experience, was most needed there.[48]

While Utkin was most likely 'advised' by the Russian state to spend most of his time in Belarus, Prigozhin was not. According to media reports, he was seen in Moscow, Saint Petersburg, and Kishinev. It is likely, that Wagner's business worldwide serving Russian state interests, as well as private business interest, would have suffered more should his travelling have been limited to Belarus, than the national security interests of the Russian state in allowing him to travel freely.

Wagner's role in Belarus was to serve two purposes. On one hand they reinforced Belorussian military capabilities, on the other hand they provided training for the Belarusian armed forces, that includes war experience. Belarus is not at war with Ukraine, even though at the initial stage of the Russian Special Military Operations the country's territory was used by Russian troops attacking Ukraine. The appearance of Wagner in Belarus caused bordering countries to become concerned, especially Ukraine. Should the war enter a new stage, Russian troops intending to take Kyiv would likely use the territory of Belarus again. Even if no offensive operations might take place using Belarussian territory, the Ukrainian Armed Forces need to station troops in the vicinity of the Belarussian border, wasting desperately needed resources on the south-eastern front.

On 3 July 2023, Prigozhin made a very interesting statement. He claimed that Wagner would return to the battlefield of the war in Ukraine 'very soon', and that, 'the internal enemy caused more damage to the PMC than the external enemy'.[49] Concerning the first part of the statement, the question arises whether Wagner would resume war-related activities from the territory of Belarus, or from somewhere else? If Prigozhin resumed war activities from Belarus, it would justify severe concerns of bordering countries, especially that of Ukraine.[50] The second half of Priogzhin's statement deserved as much attention,[51] since it sounded like the Wagner boss still believed

One of the field modifications introduced to service by the Wagner Group during the Battle of Bakhmut: a mine-roller installed on the front of a Chekan mine-resistant ambush protected (MRAP) vehicle. (via Dean O'Brien)

his ideas about an armed mutiny against the top Russian military leadership. Should those ideas have been true, it would have been a very serious issue, because he continued to play the failed and risky game against the Russian state, while the top leaders in Moscow must have been aware of that.

Prosecution

As a key part of the deal between Lukashenko and Prigozhin, resolving the Wagner armed mutiny 'without a major bloodbath', based on the authorisation and promise of Putin, the criminal charges against Prigozhin were dropped. This was the official part of the story. Since there were no official criminal charges against Prigozhin, some might have thought that he was a free person. However, that was not true. The Russian state forced him to 'cut back' his businesses in several ways. Prigozhin was forced to give up all sorts of military equipment, that spelled the end of an 'autonomously overgrown' PMC, capable of even a powerful armed mutiny against the Russian state. Having no military equipment inherited from the Ukraine war, a highly unlikely 'second try' to push through an armed mutiny against the Russian state would most likely have been rather ridiculous, than tragic.

The resulting state of Prigozhin could be best summarised in the following way: for a while after 24 June 2022, there had been 'no execution, but disgrace'; a period when Prigozhin had been 'pardoned, but not forgiven'.[52]

Prigozhin was also forced to give up his media empire.[53] Later on, the contract between the Russian Ministry of Defence and Prigozhin, that allowed Prigozhin's 'Concord Co.' to supply the Russian Military with food products,[54] was abruptly terminated by the Russian state and thus one of the most – if not the most – significant business with Wagner was terminated. All the offices of the Wagner PMC – including Prigozhin's personal one – were also searched by the Russian police, and large amounts of cash confiscated.[55] The Russian state did not go as far as to terminate the Wagner's food product businesses concerning schools and hospitals around the country, though.[56] The Russian reasoning for that suggested that there had been no problems with Wagner's food supply to schools and hospitals, and thus it was safe to continue operations of this branch of the conglomerate. Actually, and for similar reasons, there was no point in a unilateral termination of the food contract between the Russian Ministry of Defence and Wagner, initiated by the Russian MOD: this was purely a retaliation for the mutiny and to minimise the dependency of the Russian Armed Forces on Wagner, plus to decrease the PMC's income and make it incapable of any armed mutiny in the future.

Impact upon the Russian Federation

In the days following the mutiny, one of the most frequently asked questions was whether the Russian Federation would emerge from this crisis stronger or weaker. There were arguments to support or deny both conclusions.[57] An armed mutiny in itself is never a good sign for the state affected. However, the armed mutiny of Wagner showed a lot. On one hand it arose just as unexpectedly as it was resolved by negotiations. Even more importantly, the Russian top political and military leadership showed no division in agreeing the necessity to subdue the armed mutiny. Putin concluded that both the Russian people and the military were on his side, or at least they did not ask for a possible civil war, which would have caused even more damage to the country than its ongoing invasion of Ukraine:[58] that was the key to avoid bloodshed, on the one hand, and the achievement of a rapidly and successfully negotiated settlement of the armed mutiny on the other hand. Had even a few Russian brigades or regiments of the VSRF have sided with Prigozhin, the result would have been a bloodbath. Depending on how much political and military support Wagner could have possibly won, the bloodbath could have been more or less severe, but would surely have badly damaged the image and the power of the Russian state. Hundreds of the best Russian tanks and artillery pieces would have been destroyed, and personnel losses might have been prohibitively high. However, this did not happen. Thanks to Lukashenko's mediation, Putin was able to resolve the armed mutiny with a minimum number of Russian casualties; thus, his solution was probably the most effective possible. Following that, the Russian Armed Forces took virtually all of Wagner's military equipment that was used in Ukraine.

The authors' overall assessment is that the resolution of the armed mutiny based on the decisions made by the top Russian political and military leadership, especially that of president Putin, made the Russian state stronger and Wagner much weaker.[59] Russia lost six helicopters and an airplane, but it avoided all other losses and, for example, Moscow did not lose a single tank nor did it destroy Wagner's tanks. Putin's approval rating within Russia grew to above 78%.[60] Furthermore, once the OSCE Parliamentary Assembly Recognised Wagner as a terrorist organisation, an ironic Russian interpretation appeared: since the recognition followed the failed coup, it could be interpreted as 'strong support' for Putin.[61]

One of the most interesting issues was whether the external or the internal challenges of Russian statehood were more important.[62] Some experts suggested that the internal contradictions of Russia were of utmost importance, and all other contradictions secondary. The end state of the USSR was a good example for that. The USSR had not been militarily defeated by external challenges, such as lost wars, in a direct sense, even though it had to withdraw its occupation force from Afghanistan, similarly to what the US and NATO would later do, based on top level political decisions. It is far from the authors' conclusions, that external political, economic, and ultimately military, challenges from the Western world did not make a decisive contribution to the fall of the USSR. Russia (and the USSR) has appeared weak in some phases of its modern history, such as 1905, 1917, 1922, 1956, or 1989/1990, even the 1990s. The dissolution of the USSR was based on a deep internal crisis, rather than a non-existing military victory against the nuclear superpower. The USSR broke up due to top level political decisions in Moscow, that were tacitly or actively supported by wide layers of the contemporary Russian population, and also a result of a deep political confusion of the 'last bastions' of the Communist Party of the Soviet Union, the Armed Forces of the USSR, including the armed personnel under the Ministry of Internal Affairs (Internal Troops). The failed military coup against Mikhail Gorbachev was a perfect example of that, when it was unclear whether the aim of the coup was to convince him ultimately not to allow the breakup of the Soviet Union, or remove him from power, replacing him by a 'reliable' top general of the Soviet Armed Forces. We might argue whether or not giving up the Soviet empire would have benefitted Russia (the 'Russian Empire') or not, or whether it would have been sustainable or not, but that is an issue of the past and cannot much add to the assessment of the future of the Wagner Group.

In Russian circles, it is common wisdom that Russia can only be defeated by struggle of internal forces, and nothing else. So far, that appears to be applicable to the Ukraine war. A 'resource war' against Russia is a tough game, one that brought down Napoleon and Hitler, who had – relatively speaking – far superior armies of their

An MT-LB armoured personnel carrier of the Wagner Group, underway in the Bakhmut area in May 2023. (via Dean O'Brien)

time, than that of Ukrainian president Zelensky's today. However, it needs to be kept in mind, that neither Napoleon nor Hitler was supported by almost the entire West (with some simplification and generalisation).

Impact upon the War in Ukraine

Another frequently asked question was whether Wagner's mutiny had any effects upon the war in Ukraine. The brief answer in a short term was 'no', because Wagner left Bakhmut approximately two weeks prior to the armed mutiny, and the VSRF lost no terrain as a consequence. Therefore the front line of Russian defences was not affected in a short term. However, since Wagner and its structures temporarily left Russia, it was expected that the majority of the PMC would no longer be deployed in the vicinity of the Russian border. For this reason, the Wagner mutiny and its aftermath were considered as 'likely' to affect the front line between Russia and Ukraine.

As the subsequent developments were to show, no such options materialised: Wagner was re-organised into a number of smaller PMCs: all were controlled by the Ministry of Defence in Moscow, but their composition depended on preferences of their staff. Some wanted to continue serving in Ukraine, others abroad. Correspondingly, some of the resulting PMCs were returned to Ukraine and others sent to Africa, for example. Meanwhile, Wagner mercenaries were involved in training the Belarusian armed forces, including passing on up to date experience of the Ukraine war. Even though Belarus did not join Putin's invasion of Ukraine, this secured a potential point for Putin: if he decided to try taking Kyiv again, Belarus would have been used for Russian troop movement, even if the Belarusian armed forces may not become directly involved in the war.

To make things more complicated, it appears, that Wagner training bases in Crimea have been unaffected by the retaliatory measures of the Russian state against the Wagner coup. Their existence enabled deployment of well-trained soldiers during the subsequent phases of the war in Ukraine.

Potential Followers

Yet another question appearing in the aftermath of the Wagner insurrection was whether there would be possible followers, and if the Russian top military leadership was cornered. When Russian Chief of Staff, General of the Army, Valery Gerasimov took over the command (more officially and precisely, the 'supervision') of the 'Special Military Operation' in Ukraine on 11 January 2023,[63] from the Commander of Russian Aerospace Forces, General of the Army Sergey Surovikin,[64] it became immediately clear that the top Russian military leadership, including Defence Minister, General of the Army Sergey Shojgu, and General of the Army Gerasimov achieved maximum representation and responsibility in leadership of the 'Special Military Operation' in Ukraine. Leadership and coordination issues might well justify such a high representation, but it also meant that whenever a serious failure might appear during the war in Ukraine, the top Russian military leadership would not only be responsible, but they would also feel cornered. Even Vladimir Putin would feel cornered, since if his top military leadership failed in any way, he would be pressured to explain it and take decisions to correct it. Such correction could well include personal changes among the top leadership.

When General Gerasimov took over the leadership of the 'Special Military Operation' from General Surovikin, it was widely misunderstood around the world, including Russia. The interpretation of what happened allowed speculation that the Russian top military leadership was somehow unsatisfied with the performance of the former Commanding General of the 'Special Military Operation', Surovikin, thus the previous top general of the 'Special Military Operation' was 'removed' from his position. However, this was highly unlikely to be true, given that Surovikin, decorated a Hero of Russia, was not only the most talented and war-experienced Russian general, as many analysts believe, but he also did much to make the 'Special Military Operation' successful. In a short time, following Surovikin's takeover, significant improvements occurred concerning previously widely criticised supply and discipline issues, the massive use of all sorts of drones was introduced, and following the first explosion of the Kerch bridge on 9 October 2022,[65] it was Surovikin who organised and executed the massive, precision bombardment of the Ukrainian critical energy infrastructure, especially electric network capabilities such as generation, transformation, balancing, and transportation. Surovikin dared to push through the shortening of the overall length

Wreckage of (from left to right) an MT-LB armoured personnel carrier, a BTR-82A armoured personnel carrier, and two BMP-2 infantry fighting vehicles of the Wagner Group, knocked out during the fighting in the Opytne area, in April 2023. (ZSU)

of the front line, that resulted in improved effectiveness, but also in territorial losses, including the Russian withdrawal from right bank of the Dnieper, loosing part of Kherson region. The latter was a highly unpopular action based on Russian public opinion, widely over-politicised, criticised, and misunderstood, but from the Russian military point of view it was a necessary decision. The immense Russian defensive lines – protected by up to 20-kilometres-deep belt of minefields – which have successfully withstood the Ukrainian counteroffensive are also called the 'Surovikin Defensive Line',[66] since they were built following the general's concept and orders. Many analysts believe, that the bloody 'meat grinder' in Bakhmut was also Surovikin's idea to bleed the Ukrainians through Russian air and artillery superiority. Removing such a commanding general from the 'Special Military Operation' was a questionable decision, even if keeping him in a lower command position, and suggests speculation that the top Russian military leadership has even been jealous of his outstanding performance.

Immediately following the armed mutiny of Wagner, General Surovikin rightly addressed Prigozhin and his soldiers on 24 June 2023.[67] Following that day Surovikin vanished, making no further public appearances.[68] Some sources suggested, that he was arrested on suspicion of being part of Wagner's armed mutiny,[69] others suggested, that he was on holiday at an unspecified location.[70] Whatever happened, both Surovikin and the Russian top military leadership were silent about his fate for a while after. Since Surovikin was not only assigned to be second in command of the 'Special Military Operation', he was also the Commanding General of the Russian Aerospace Forces, once the fate of such a top general becomes unclear, it suggests both serious problems within the top level of the Russian chain of command, and also handling the issue concerning public communications. Eventually, Surovikin re-surfaced and on 10 September 2023 was unanimously elected head of the Coordinating Committee for Air Defence under the Council of the Commonwealth of Indpendent States. Ever since, he has visited Africa – including Algeria – on a number of occasions, promptly ending all speculations about his fate: he continued formally balancing between both the Russian Ministry of Defence, and the post-Wagner PMCs.

In turn this is making it clear that Surovikin never failed to follow the orders of the Russian Ministry of Defence. In turn, it is theoretically possible, that Surovikin knew about the mutiny of Prigozhin, since they maintained a close relationship, but had not reported about it in a timely manner: this is what is likely to have cost him Putin's and the trust by the top Russian military leadership.

Popov's Removal

The sacking of Major General Ivan Popov, Commanding General of the Russian 58th Combined Arms Army (CAA), defending the key Zaporozhe region of the eastern front in Ukraine, potentially a key for the success or failure of a Ukrainian counterattack, occurred on 12 July 2023. General Popov was removed by Chief of Staff, Army General Gerasimov, that raised a lot of 'dust' in Russia.[71] Popov's private report was made public on 13 July 2023 by the Deputy Chairman of the Russian State Duma's Defence Committee, Lieutenant General (Ret.) Andrey Grulev, a Member of Parliament, and it contained very serious allegations. The original reports made by General Popov were not published, but his audio message, where he commented upon his removal from position, was. Since it was an audio message originally made for colleges, it was not the leaking a classified document, therefore General Grulev was unlikely to be held criminally liable for making it public. In the audio message, General Popov was very sincere and tough. He described his relationship with his subordinates, and also the situation in which he either insists his truth or hide, saying things that top military leaders wanted to hear in the Russian Ministry of Defence. He decided to call the problems what they were, and to stand up for his subordinates dying in unnecessarily high numbers due to failures of the Russian Ministry of Defence.[72] The military shortcomings, that Popov listed, included inadequate counterbattery activities and reconnaissance against the Ukrainian armed forces.

Analysing Popov's statements from that message is in turn helping clarify the nature of Russian military shortcomings that are not obvious for those not professional in this field of expertise. Inadequate counterbattery activities on the Russian side were hard to believe at first glance, even though several Russian experts referred to them almost on a permanent basis, simply quoting the issue, but failing to explain its reasons. It was difficult to accept, since the two most frequently quoted Russian superiorities on the eastern front of Ukraine were in air and artillery. According to the contemporary Commander-in-Chief of the ZSU, General Valery Zaluzhny, Russian artillery capabilities exceed those of the Ukrainian Army tenfold.[73] A major shortcoming concerning Russian counterbattery activities was thus not related to the lack of artillery pieces and ammunition, but equipment, training, and procedures. For example: the artillery radars, the lack of their digital interconnectedness and lack of a unified, computer-supported decision-making system, where data coming from other reconnaissance sources was also considered. It was not enough, if a counterbattery radar picked up the coordinates of enemy artillery pieces, and the nearby field artillery guns fired at those targets, because the battery conducting the counterbattery fire had to be ideally placed and supplied with ammunition. If firing orders were not distributed ideally to the artillery batteries, and reconnaissance data was not properly integrated, the effectiveness of counterbattery fire and also the utilisation of up-to-date reconnaissance and intelligence data was compromised. If the distribution of firing missions within counterbattery warfare was not ideal between artillery batteries, the result was that some fire missions have missed due to excessive firing ranges, other fire missions were never tasked to batteries that were within range, there was a lack of ammunition, and too much exposure to the enemy counterbattery fire. In turn, this was why the Ukrainian military, despite experiencing a lack of ammunition or artillery pieces but building their counterbattery warfare capability not only through the utilisation of individual counterbattery radars, but through more up to date rules of coordination and cooperation – taken from Western field manuals, thanks to Western instructors – was relatively more effective.

This was a conclusion by the authors' based on field artillery studies at the United States Field Artillery Officers' Advanced Course, as well as broad field artillery studies and experience stretching back to the Warsaw Pact era. In case of the Russian army, their practices in the Warsaw Pact era can still be witnessed, similarly to that in Ukraine. Both military cultures put a great emphasis on the use of field artillery and use excessive amounts of artillery ammunition, that remains only partially understandable for those following strictly Western manuals. Concerning the artillery standards of the armies of the former Warsaw Pact, based on Soviet field manuals, one of the greatest challenges was the high percentage of fire missions (up to 70–80%) unobserved by observation posts and other reconnaissance units or assets, leading to excessively high usage of field artillery ammunition while also lacking effectiveness. Such a military culture still remains in the Russian and – to a lesser degree – in Ukrainian army, essentially having the same roots in military culture and it is having far reaching consequences, since a proper supply of field artillery ammunition for the Ukrainian army remains one of major difficulties both for Kyiv and the West. In turn, such conditions – based on excessive use of military resources – remain advantageous for the Russian armed forces, with the potential to seriously affect the outcome of the war in Ukraine.

In addition to shortcomings concerning Russian counterbattery warfare and reconnaissance, General Popov also drew attention to the lack of rotation of Russian units, due to their significant losses in combat. At first glance, this appeared to be a purely organisational issue, where the top level Russian military leadership failed to do its duty. Should an army, such as the 58th CAA, formerly under the command of General Popov, need such rotations, the responsibility of higher echelons of command are evident. However, this is clearly not a purely organisational issue, since it required higher echelons to accept the true Russian losses on the ground that would be a prerequisite to making decisions concerning the rotation of units that had suffered significant losses. Should higher echelons of Russian military leadership fail to accept the number of casualties of particular units along the front line, the higher echelons of command would also tend to ignore requests for rotation. Such a theory perfectly fits the picture of unfair management practices in the higher echelons of Russian military command, far above the 58th CAA. Should it be true, it was unfair, because failure to rotate leads to further, unnecessary casualties on the front on one hand, and on the other hand it obscures the real number of casualties suffered by Russian forces from President Putin. Of course, the situation is not as simple as it may first appear, since rotation of units suffering significant casualties would have to be achieved based on the resources of the Russian 58th CAA. However, when, at the level of the 58th CAA, the possibilities of such rotations are reduced, a crisis follows, and the authors tend to believe that this is exactly what happened when General Popov started insisting to the higher echelons upon rotation. Should this be true, it would fully explain why General Popov tried to resist the wrong approach and decisions by higher echelons of command. This led Popov into a process where he started performing a kind of 'suicide mission' with his own personnel carrier, attempting to save his subordinate soldiers that were losing effectiveness in a critical time during the Ukrainian counteroffensive. Should this theory be true, it would also perfectly explain why General Popov insisted on his fair relationship with his subordinates, that support promised by him would remain following his dismissal from the position of the Commanding General of the Russian 58th CAA. Should that support continue, which was a fair pledge on the part of the Russian general, it would never be the same in comparison to what he could do when in position as the commanding general of the 58th CAA. However, it is a difficult issue to evaluate, because General Popov could not insist on protecting his subordinates against the wrong decisions of higher echelons of the Russian military command, and his ability to save his subordinates to a necessary and fair extent would have vanished anyway. Should it be true, his 'mutiny-like' resignation was absolutely understandable. What has been analysed here also perfectly fits the 'strange war' model discussed earlier in this text, referring to lack of rotation of troops.

In addition to military shortcomings and the resulting unnecessary casualties on the Russian side, Popov accused Gerasimov of 'Decapitating the army at the most difficult and tense moment, our supreme commander struck us from behind in a treacherous and vile manner.'[74] Anyone who communicated this certainly could not expect to be appointed to a new position to which General Gerasimov would add his name, unless ordered by Putin to pardon Popov, and thus resolve the over-politicised conflict. All Russian sources, with few exceptions, wrote only good things about Popov and described his dismissal as 'unworthy' and 'unjust'. Those who abstained from praising Popov, claimed that he was not a general who determined the policies (or the 'face') of the 'Special Military Operation' and therefore his departure from the position of the Commanding General of the 58th CAA would not affect the performance of the Russian Armed Forces in Ukraine.[75] Sources loyal to General Popov claim that the development of the drone capabilities of the 58th CAA was his achievement without the support of the Russian military top management, allegedly even against their will, and which did much to strengthen Russian defences. According to one analyst, such a person should not be expelled from his position but be awarded the title of Hero of Russia (the highest military honour in Russia).

The charges made by General Popov against the top Russian military leadership were very similar to those of Prigozhin. It seems that the goal was to oust Shoigu and Gerasimov, the very same as what Prigozhin wanted to achieve. Popov would have been ready to report to Putin personally, but he did not get that far.[76] According to him, this was the ultimate reason of his dismissal from the position of the Commanding General of the 58th CAA in Ukraine. The general confirmed the news of his own dismissal, unlike the most famous, talented and effective contemporary Russian general, General Sergey Surovikin, who may have been under arrest since the Prigozhin coup.

General Popov's 'mutiny' followed Wagner's armed mutiny in a relatively short time and could be called as such in a political and military professional sense, but was not a mutiny in strictly legal terms.

A mercenary of the Wagner Group in Soledar, March 2023. (via Dean O'Brien)

A knocked out Chekan MRAP of the Wagner Group, seen abandoned in the Bakhmut area, in August 2023. (via Dean O'Brien)

Wagner's Potential Role in the ultimate Resolution of the War in Ukraine

This section analyses three possible major strategic outcomes of the Ukraine war.

According to the first scenario, Ukraine might win the war with lasting and massive Western financial and military support, regaining all of its territories. Such an outcome of the war might enable Ukraine to become a member of NATO and the EU – all provided that some form of a peace agreement would be reached with Russia in order to end the territorial conflict with Moscow. Should there be no peace agreement and a convincingly effective ceasefire at the Russian-Ukrainian border, and should Ukraine become a member of NATO, a direct NATO-Russia war remains a risk. Should Article V operations be required in resolving the armed conflict, it would mean entering a direct armed conflict with Russia, that is, a NATO-Russia war.[77]

Should a NATO-Russia war become reality, it would likely become nuclear and it would likely spell the end of humanity as we know it, if not entirely. Should the war become nuclear, there would likely be no winners and losers. The loser would be humanity as a whole, since there are two nuclear superpowers, the United States of America and the Russian Federation, and it should be kept in mind that both nuclear superpowers have more than enough nuclear capabilities do destroy human life on Earth.[78] Should Article V not be included in peace settlement efforts, it could indeed seriously discredit what is probably the most important cornerstone of NATO.[79] Humanity might survive, Russia would not go nuclear, but people around the world would see Article V discredited, since it would not be applied against a nuclear superpower. Even though this part of the analysis, that details the risks of NATO enlargement in case of Ukraine is not widely propagated in the Western world, its validity is indirectly proven by the clarification of both NATO Secretary General Jens Stoltenberg, and US President Joe Biden, who confirm that Ukraine is unfit to join NATO while in a state of war with Russia, especially if Kyiv was not the winner of the war.[80] According to a basic document the Alliance, the *Study on NATO Enlargement* (1995), this set of problems is well understood: 'States which have ethnic disputes or external territorial disputes, including irredentist claims, or internal jurisdictional disputes must settle those disputes by peaceful means in accordance with OSCE principles. Resolution of such disputes would be a factor in determining whether to invite a state to join the Alliance.'[81]

It should also be kept in mind that should it become a serious possibility that Ukraine was close to regaining all or most lost territories, some being part of Russia according to the Russian Constitution, Moscow would likely resort to tactical nuclear weapons. According to the Russian nuclear doctrine,[82] loss of Russian territories, a major threat against the statehood, or the State's inability to overcome military threat, empower the president to decide to use nuclear weapons, even against a non-nuclear state, such as Ukraine as we know it. That would spell the end of Ukrainian military successes, and the country would likely be depopulated, become uninhabitable, and lose its statehood in any meaningful sense. Since Kyiv has admitted that Ukrainian counteroffensives have not achieved any significant territorial gains, the loss of significant Russian territories in favour of Ukraine is not yet in sight.

A possible terrorist attack at the Zaporozhye nuclear power plant[83] could well be equal to the effects of a dirty bomb, or it could even be worse than Chernobyl. The authors consider it unlikely that Russia may resort to nuclear terrorism against a nuclear power plant under Russian control.[84] According to Kyiv, Russia has prepared remote detonation of the used fuel rods of the Zaporozhye power plant to create a dirty bomb effect, in order to stop a Ukrainian armed offensive if retaining Russian control of the nuclear power plant becomes impossible. Meanwhile, Russia has blamed Kyiv in advance, claiming that Ukraine has planned acts of nuclear terrorism. Should such, or similar, events occur, the Russian bombardment of the top decision makers in Kyiv (president, government, parliament, MOD, MoFA, SBU) would be highly likely, and the Russian use of tactical nuclear weapons would likely be closer. The authors consider this scenario highly unlikely, since it assumes total regaining of lost territories that Ukraine, as we know it, is not capable of.[85]

It is important to stress, that 'Ukraine, as we know it,' is not capable of regaining all, or at least most, of the territories lost to Russia. Such a statement leaves open the possibility of a major strengthening of Ukrainian military capabilities, at least in theory. For those not convinced, the authors suggest considering the date and the scope of the Ukrainian counteroffensive. The first announcement of the counteroffensive came in autumn 2022. Then it was predicted for winter 2022. Then for spring 2023, and finally it started in summer 2023. The scope of the Ukrainian counteroffensive was to regain lost territories, including Crimea, and force the Russians to negotiate a peace agreement from position of power on Kyiv's side. However, the 2023 Ukrainian counteroffensive failed to regain any strategically measurable land,[86] while Russian defences in Ukraine, including the world's largest minefields, proved to be lasting and effective.[87] Having no Ukrainian superiority over Russia in field artillery or in the air,[88] the Ukrainian counteroffensive was doomed to failure at the core of its concept. No matter whose field manuals we might decide to study, including former Soviet Army manuals, the attacking party must be superior to the defender in order to successfully perform offensive military operations. Should Ukraine not be superior militarily all along the Russian defensive lines, that is approximately 800 kilometres, it must have the mentioned superiority at least locally, where Kyiv expected the success of the Ukrainian counteroffensive to materialise. This is why it is important to keep in mind, that the authors are analysing the current power ratio between Ukraine and Russia, and not only Ukrainian military capabilities of the foreseeable future, but that could also change. It could change in favour of Kyiv, or in favour of Moscow: our respected readers might decide which path has a greater chance of becoming reality.

It should also be taken into consideration, that – especially politicians and key generals – tend to confuse various types of Ukrainian military victories over Russia, leading them to unsubstantiated and incorrect conclusions. At least three types of Ukrainian military victories over Russia can be taken into consideration.

The first type could be the destruction of the flagship of the Russian Black Sea Fleet by Ukraine or similar successful attacks against Russian targets. No doubt, the sinking of *Moskva* was a classic victory on the Ukrainian part, that should not be debated at all.

The second type of Ukrainian military victory could involve regaining territories that the Russian Armed forces abandoned based on top level political and military decisions made by the Kremlin and the Russian Ministry of Defence. Such Russian decisions were officially communicated as efforts to save the lives of Russian soldiers and were very unpopular with mainstream Russian public, leading to confusion and multiple debates whether these actions could be considered the results of right or wrong decisions. No doubt, that these would also be classic Ukrainian military victories over Russia, and even the pace of regaining Ukrainian territories was impressive. However, the nuance is that in these cases there was a form of 'active Russian consent' to allow Ukrainian military victories, rather than sacrificing Russian soldiers under conditions undesirable for Moscow. The Russian decision to withdraw from the vicinity of Kyiv was the first example of this, but Kharkov or Kherson could also be mentioned, where similar Russian withdrawals occurred. It should be kept in mind that these events have already occurred, since General of the Army Sergey Surovikin consolidated Russian defence lines along the eastern front in Ukraine in terms of the numbers of personnel, discipline, logistics, planting of minefields, and shortening the length of the front line. Thus, the realities suggest, that the second type of Ukrainian military victory will no longer be part of the war in Ukraine.

There is a third type of Ukrainian military victory over Russia, where Russian armed forces prepare their defensive lines and insist upon holding them. This type of Ukrainian victory exists only in theory in strategic terms. The results of the Ukrainian counteroffensives to date are proof of that so far. Should Ukraine be able to show this third type of victory at the strategic level, that would be a very significantly different ballgame to what was seen in autumn 2023. Claims by Russian politicians that the 'Special Military Operation' has gone according to the plans is a lie exposed by many analysts. Similarly, suggestions by Kyiv, that the Ukrainian counteroffensive went to plan is a severe distortion of the nature of the realities on the ground. Politicians and top generals tend to provide hope and encouragement to their people, including the soldiers fighting on the front lines on both sides, rather than honestly admitting their own failures, thus damaging morale. However, neither politicians, nor top generals can escape responsibility for what they say and what they do. Leading a nation to a strategically unsuccessful counteroffensive, that creates unjustified casualty levels on the Ukrainian side speaks for itself.

According to the second scenario, the war's outcome is a kind of a stalemate, when Ukraine loses territories in the long run, but none of the parties can significantly change the borders and there is enough will to stop the war.[89] In the event of a peace settlement signed under such conditions, both Russia and Ukraine would claim it as a victory. In this case, nuclear scenarios appear to be averted, at least for a while. However, the major problem with this scenario is that, as of now, none of the parties is willing to seriously negotiate, intending to resolve the conflict purely on their own terms. The 'peace formula' of Zelensky goes even further than regaining all of the lost territories of Ukraine. It demands punishment of the Russian leaders involved in the war, and payment of war reparations by the Russian state to rebuild Ukraine. In Ukraine there is even a law prohibiting any negotiations with Putin's state leaders. Such demands are unrealistic given the popularity and power of Putin.

According to NATO Secretary General Jens Stoltenberg and several other leaders, NATO membership of Ukraine has a prerequisite, that is victory over Russia. Should victory not be achieved, as witnessed in the second scenario, NATO membership would not be achieved either. Even if this scenario might take place, it is likely to follow the fate of the Minsk Agreements, when none of the parties had a true will to comply with the agreements. Understandingly, such a context did not result in a lasting peace, but rather a frozen conflict was created, resulting in casualties on a regular basis on both sides. Should Ukraine lose more territories than in case of the Minsk Agreements, and receive more political, financial and military support (handing over intel data,[90] training,

ZSU unit patches taken as trophies, captured by Wagner operatives, mainly during the fighting in the Bakhmut area in 2022–2023. (via Dean O'Brien)

provision of weapons and ammunition, for example) from the West, the more frustration would likely accumulate to somehow continue the war and recover the lost territories. In other words, there will unlikely be lasting peace based on this outcome, and the resumption of the full-scale war will likely be only a question of time.

Such a scenario is likely in the short and even the medium term, but it is unlikely in the long run due to tendencies never allowing to achieve a lasting peace.

According to the third scenario, the war's outcome would be the destruction of Ukrainian statehood as we know it,[91] and the war either ends with a total Russian victory, gaining control of Ukraine as a whole, or the remaining parts of Ukraine might be divided between Russia and other states, such as Poland. Some experts argue that the divisions between Kyiv and Warsaw are so deep, that the two countries might not come to an agreement on a kind of a joint statehood. Other experts argue that Russia will not tolerate a serious Polish intervention in Ukraine, even if it is welcomed by Kyiv. Others suggest that a division of Ukraine would not be politically appropriate, therefore would not be approved by NATO and EU, and thus impossible.[92]

Should Russia control the entire territory of Ukraine as a result of the war, a key issue will arise: the fate of the Ukrainian population.[93] Should the vast majority of Ukrainian nationals leave the country because of destruction resulting from the war, including not only the threat against their lives, but also lack of working opportunities and miserable living conditions, Russia might afford to accommodate all Ukrainian territories as part of Russia. Former Russian president and prime minister, Dmitry Medvedev suggested, that no anti-Russian state should survive, that especially concerns Ukraine,[94] while many key Russian politicians, including Putin, have made it clear that the scope of the 'Special Military Operation' (such as demilitarisation, denazification, elimination of threats against Russia) covers the entirety of Ukraine.

Should tens of millions of Ukrainian nationals, desperately opposing Russian occupation, remain in Ukraine, the full victory of Moscow would likely tend towards a total defeat, when Russia would continuously pay the price of occupying territories to a point where only its withdrawal would resolve the situation. It is likely, that vast majority of the Ukrainian population would leave Ukraine in this scenario due to the war and for social reasons and would never come back. Those eager to seriously resist Russian occupation would likely be either killed or expelled from the country.

Even though most experts and politicians in the Western world do not believe in such a scenario, the authors suggest that this is the most likely scenario, even if not realised in the short term. The reason is that it is very difficult to win resource wars against Russia, and the Western support for Ukraine would likely be limited in one way or another. Furthermore, whatever Western support Ukraine would get, it would sooner or later have to exclusively rely on it, since the Soviet/Russian types of weaponry and ammunition will be depleted completely. The authors suggest that Ukrainian vs. Russian demographics will play a major role in the outcome of the war, with a bottleneck on the Ukrainian side. There are also reasons to believe that, sooner or later, Russia would push the Ukrainian economy into a non-functional status, i.e. by further destruction of its critical energy infrastructure. Properly explaining all these factors goes beyond the scope of our analysis.

4
CRITICAL PERCEPTION OF THE WAGNER GROUP

Such a wide range of possible utilisation of the Wagner Group by definition raises serious questions concerning legal aspects of their activities and generates criticism of other political, economic and military influencers, especially if they view Russia as a competitor or even an adversary. Mainstream politicians and media usually tend to view Russian influence in a critical way,[1] especially if it is associated with utilisation of military force abroad. According to this logic, the mainstream finds multiple reasons to discredit the Wagner Group.

One of the main negative arguments was – and remains – the claim that war crimes had been committed by the Wagner Group all around the world, and that the cruelty of their mercenaries is partially due to the fact that a huge percentage of their fighters are in fact former prisoners, recruited with the promise that following their service detailed in their half-year-long contract, they would be pardoned by the Russian President. Even Russian pro-Wagner sources admitted that by the late 2023, a little under half of the Wagner Group was comprised of former prisoners.[2]

However, for the Russian state there are advantages as well. On one hand, should the former prisoner mercenaries fall, they are not members of the Russian Armed Forces, thereby their number as casualties need not be accounted for by the Russian state. On the other hand, the former prisoners have a very specific, but powerful motivation to keep the rules of the Wagner Group, thereby strictly following the orders of their commanders.

The main principles of the Wagner Group were the following:[3]

1. Protect the interests of Russia always and everywhere.
2. The honour of a Russian fighter is above all.
3. Fight not for money, but out of principle! And the principle is one – victory.
4. Do not surrender to enemies alive! If you are captured, die, but take as many lives of enemies as possible with you.
5. Honour your dead comrades. Do not bring shame to their bright memory. You will meet them sooner or later.
6. For us, death awaits on the battlefield and not in the bed of a weak old man.
7. Help a friend in battle. Today you covered him, tomorrow he will cover you.
8. Be humble and don't brag about your profession, keep this secret.
9. Never loot.
10. At war and at home – do not drink.
11. At war and at home – do not use drugs.
12. Don't steal, don't rob, don't rape.
13. Do not kill civilians.
14. Keep your dog tag, remember: you are a Wagner PMC fighter.

At its high point in late 2022, mercenaries of the Wagner Group were manning an entire squadron of the VKS equipped with Su-24M fighter-bombers. This photograph shows the left side and the fin of one of the aircraft in question. Notable is the miscellany of weaponry loaded on the aircraft, including bombs ranging from 50kg to 250kg. (Russian social media)

In addition to Su-24s and Su-25s, mercenaries of the Wagner Group are known to have manned at least one squadron of Mi-8AMTSh assault helicopters, one of which is seen behind this group of contractors. (Russian social media)

According to pro-Wagner Russian sources training and discipline in the Wagner Group were tough but fair. Whenever mercenaries failed to obey the rules outlined in their contract, they were either killed if they betrayed the Wagner Group or sent back to prison if they did some less serious 'mischief'. Wagner Group members considered themselves 'brothers', and that was not an exaggeration: they fought on some of the toughest battlefields: if they failed to see each other as 'brothers', they would likely have suffered even heavier casualties. This was a general logic of survival that went beyond military manuals. Russian pro-Wagner sources suggested that most former prisoners gained discipline by serving in the Wagner Group and became 'truly different people', eligible to be pardoned. Several personal interviews suggested the same.[4] Putin's supporters tended to emphasise the officially acknowledged connection between the Russian state and the Wagner Group,[5] viewing their members as extremely well-trained heroes who risked their lives for the Motherland. It should be noted that there is a tendency stemming from the Russian head of state to enhance the legal status of the mercenaries of the Wagner Group providing them with similar, or the same, rights as those of Russian soldiers employed directly by the state, i.e., the benefits of a veteran status. However, there is also an opposite tendency to keep the legal status of Wagner in a grey zone.

A mercenary of the Wagner Group inside a ruined church in Soledar, March 2023. (via Dean O'Brien)

Former ZSU positions in completely ruined Soledar. (via Dean O'Brien)

The mission of the Wagner Group based on an analysis of Prigozhin's comments

Prigozhin's comments on the 'historic role' of the Wagner Group have recently appeared in social media and were picked up by Russian media.[6] His thoughts deserve an analysis because they included exaggerations, typical of promotion of the PMC, competition and frustration with the Russian Armed Forces. Furthermore, they added to the fog of war, and could even have been interpreted as encouragement (or bait) for the Ukrainian Armed Forces to go ahead with their planned and widely propagated counteroffensive.

> The Bakhmut meat grinder is a historical battle where the armed forces of Ukraine were practically destroyed, but, unfortunately, the Wagner PMC was also not weakly battered. In the battle between Ukraine and the collective West on the one hand, and Russia with a small number of allies on the other, the general battle of Wagner PMC against the Armed Forces of Ukraine, in which the Orchestra will win, will be the greatest turning point in this war and in all modern history, Prigozhin stressed. Because only one Russian Army will remain on the chessboard, and all other pieces will be removed from it. And if the Wagner PMC dies in the Bakhmut meat grinder and takes the Armed Forces of Ukraine and the forces attached to it with foreign weapons, and gives the Russian Army the opportunity to go further, then Wagner will fulfil its historical role. But for this, everyone else must not click [with fingers], everyone else must be ready and go forward.[7]

When reading Prigozhin's comment, the impression is often created that the Wagner Group fought the Ukrainian armed forces entirely alone. However, because Prigozhin's PMC was financed by the Russian state and got most weaponry, ammunition and equipment from the Russian military, furthermore, the Russian armed forces closely cooperated with the PMC not only during the 'Special Military Operation' in Ukraine, but earlier too (Luhansk, Donbas, Syria) it was unrealistic to claim that the Wagner Group fought alone.[8] Although the Ukrainian armed forces suffered a defeat in Bahmut, it was a great exaggeration to suggest that it was equal to their complete defeat. It is strange that Prigozhin wrote about Wagner's historical role while meaning solely its role in Ukraine, since the Wagner Group was still present in many countries, in its role around the globe.

Acknowledging significant Wagner casualties was a sensitive issue, especially during an unfinished war. However, it made sense if it discouraged further Ukrainian war efforts in the Bakhmut 'meat grinder', assuming that the Russian political and military leadership was fully aware of the nature of the conflict and understood that this was more evidently a war of attrition. Thus, Ukrainian military efforts to keep Bakhmut served Russian goals well: the battle caused unsustainable casualties to the Ukrainian side due to Russian artillery superiority, thereby effectively weakening the capabilities of Kyiv.

Wagner's Legacy in Modern-Day Russian Armed Forces

Of particular interest were recommendations that the entire Russian military should be transformed based on the principles of the Wagner Group.[9] At first look, keeping in mind that the average Wagner mercenary was far better trained, motivated, equipped, experienced and paid than the average Russian soldier, such calls were understandable and reasonable. That said, the VSRF eventually followed other aspects of Wagner's experience – primarily by recruiting convicts from Russian prisons, and then 'spending' them as 'disposable infantry' during assaults on ZSU positions.

Indeed, at least since it resumed its offensive operations in the Avdiivka sector in autumn 2023, the Russian Ground Forces integrated the majority of the lessons learned by the Wagner Group

Wreckage of Ukrainian vehicles in a field west of Bakhmut, seen in late March 2023. (via Dean O'Brien)

at the tactical level. Most of their motor-rifle formations were reorganised into infantry platoons of 12–15 soldiers, supported by armoured vehicles and dedicated fire support.

In turn, the Storm-Z detachments were usually organised into battalions, each of three companies of around 100 combatants, each with four 10-man capture squads, four 10-man fire-support squads, an 8-man reconnaissance squad, a five-man engineer squad, three-man medical evacuation squad, a two-person command element, and a two-person UAV section. Most of the Storm-Z battalions are controlled by brigade or divisional headquarters, but their elements assigned to lower-level units as necessary.

Usually, two such assault platoons working in coordination were assigned a Storm-Z detachment of convicts, serving as 'disposable infantry' used to advance and identify Ukrainian defensive positions, in turn enabling more capable forces to engage. At the time of writing, Storm-Z detachments remain the spearheads of every major Russian assault in the Ukraine War.

5
CONCLUSIONS

On 23 August 2023, Prigozhin and nine other top commanders of the Wagner PMC – including the co-founder Dmitry Utkin – were killed in a 'mysterious' aircraft crash, as his private jet was underway from Moscow to Saint Petersburg. Death of the passengers was officially confirmed four days later, following genetic analysis of the bodies recovered from the wreckage. A Wagner-associated Telegram channel claimed the jet was shot down by Russian air defences over the Tver Oblast.[1]

Notwithstanding what could be described as an inevitable end of this PMC, the fact is that over the last 20 years we have witnessed a global renaissance of PMCs.[2] The Wagner Group was one of the most powerful PMCs in the world before the failed armed mutiny that resulted in its complete disarmament, reorganisation and public subordination to the Ministry of Defence in Moscow. The Wagner Group's operating principles were based on the same or similar principles to other PMCs, including Western ones.[3] With its fate sealed, it is highly unlikely that this PMC would ever regain the power and influence that it had prior to the failed coup. However, it does not mean that the place of Wagner would not be filled by some other Russian PMCs or other, foreign PMCs, depending on the mission. It is also likely, that the Russian state would never again allow any PMC to grow to become as Wagner was prior the armed mutiny. It is a lesson learnt for the Kremlin to make sure that no other mutiny can be possible again, performed by Wagner, or any other PMC.

PMCs allow states to influence high level politics, gain economic advantage in various countries while operating in a sort of 'grey zone', maintaining different levels of deniability and ambiguity. PMCs are even capable of fighting wars, while their casualties are treated differently to those of regular armies: politicians are not pressured to take responsibility or account for PMC casualties. PMCs also have a better than average chance to escape the legal consequences of their illegal activities, including harming civilians.

A particularity of the Wagner Group to employ convicted personnel (not necessarily serving their prison terms) has allowed Russia to convert a sort of burden to a valuable asset serving the strategic goals of Russian state interests and also serving Russian business interests. As a result of changes to the legal background, the Russian armed forces are also allowed to contract convicted personnel, even if those convicted had not been involved in 'serious' crimes. Thus, the Russian armed forces are in a position now to fill the vacuum left by the disarmed contingent of Wagner that served in Ukraine. It should also be taken into consideration that disarmed Wagner personnel will likely contract to the Russian military on an individual basis, as required by the legal background created by the Russian Ministry of Defence.

In the case of the Wagner Group, Russian state interests and private business interests were thoroughly interconnected, creating a self-sustaining symbiosis prior to the failed coup. The era of such a well-operating symbiosis is over and it is highly unlikely, that anything similar will ever return. In the case of Russian PMCs, it is highly likely that the role of Wagner would be replaced by many other PMCs, performing their tasks in parallel. It is also highly likely, that great powers being able to afford financing and training well equipped, quasi 'elite' PMCs will gain significant advantages in armed conflicts around the world.

Yunus-Bek Yevkurov (left) and Andrey Troshev, who assumed responsibility for the Afrika Korps: the re-organised remnants of the former Wagner PMC, nowadays directly and openly controlled by the GRU and the Ministry of Defence in Moscow. (Wagner PMC)

Aside from memorabilia and official records, the Wagner PMC no longer exists. However, its legacy endures – not only through the tactics adopted by the Russian Ground Forces in the ongoing war in Ukraine but also through its former military commanders and thousands of veterans, who now serve in successor PMCs and the Russian Armed Forces. (Wagner PMC)

ENDNOTES

Chapter 1

1. Jones Seth G. Jones, Catrina Doxsee, Brian Katz, Eric McQueen and Joe Moye, 'Russia's Corporate Soldiers, The Global Expansion of Russia's Private Military Companies,' *Center for Strategic and International Studies (CSIS), A Report of the CSIS Transnational Threats Project*, July, 2021, p. 28.
2. Liza Reznikova, 'Donbass menyayet Rossiyu, ona stanovitsya drugoy'. 'Antifashist' pogovoril s Sergeyem Zakharchenko, synom pervogo glavy DNR,' *Antifashist*, April 4, 2023, https://antifashist.com/item/donbass-menyaet-rossiyu-ona-stanovitsya-drugoj-antifashist-pogovoril-s-sergeem-zaharchenko-synom-pervogo-glavy-dnr.html, accessed: 4 April 2023; Gwendolyn Sasse, *The Crimea Question* (Harvard University Press, Ukrainian Studies, 2007), pp. 7, 107–126, 224–225, 236, 268–269.
3. '*Russia; Ukraine: Legislature Adopts Law on Dissolution of Black Sea Fleet Treaties,*' Library of Congress, 2023, https://www.loc.gov/item/global-legal-monitor/2014-04-03/russia-ukraine-legislature-adopts-law-on-dissolution-of-black-sea-fleet-treaties/; Tyler Felgenhauer, 'Ukraine, Russia, and the Black Sea Fleet Accords,' Defense Technical Information Center, February 1, 1999, https://apps.dtic.mil/sti/citations/ADA360381; Philippe Conde, Vasco Martins, 'Russia's Black Sea fleet in Sevastopol beyond 2017,' *Diploweb*, May 23, 2010, https://www.diploweb.com/Russia-s-Black-Sea-fleet-in.html; Soglasheniye mezhdu Rossiyskoy Federatsiyey i Ukrainoy o statuse i usloviyakh prebyvaniya Chernomorskogo flota Rossiyskoy Federatsii na territorii Ukrainy (Kiyev, 28 maya 1997 g.) (s izmeneniyami i dopolneniyami) (ne deystvuyet),' *Garant*, 2023, https://base.garant.ru/1148072/, accessed: March 20, 2023.
4. Kimberly Marten, 'Russia's use of semi-state security forces: the case of the Wagner Group,' *Post-Soviet Affairs* 35, no. 3 (2019), pp. 12–13, DOI: 10.1080/1060586X.2019.1591142; Andreas Heinemann-Grüder, Stephen Aris, *Russian Analytical Digest*, no. 290, ETH Zurich, December 22, 2022, pp. 2–3, https://doi.org/10.3929/ethz-b-000588677.
5. 'Russia's use of its private military companies', *Strategic Comments* 26, no. 10 (2020), vii–viii, 3. DOI: 10.1080/13567888.2020.1868812.
6. Cooper et all, *War in Ukraine, Vol.2*, pp. 41-44, 45-50, 52-53; Cooper et all, *War in Ukraine, Vol.6*, pp. 47-50, 53-56, 60-61, 63, 77-78, 80-83 & Matters, *War in Ukraine, Vol.8* (to be published in March 2025).
7. Benoît Vitkine, 'The political ambitions of Russia's Wagner Group boss, Yevgeny Prigozhin – known for his 'troll factories' responsible for electoral interference – is preparing to launch a conservative movement', *Le Monde*, 18 November 2022, https://www.lemonde.fr/en/international/article/2022/11/18/the-political-ambitions-of-russia-s-wagner-group-boss_6004751_4.html, accessed: 20 July 2023; Maria Katarmadze, 'Who is Yevgeny Prigozhin, the man who challenged Putin?, The owner of the Wagner private military contractor and leader of a massive internet troll farm called for an armed rebellion to oust Russia's defense minister. But is he a threat to President Vladimir Putin?' *Deutsche Welle*, 25 June 2023, https://www.dw.com/en/who-is-yevgeny-prigozhin-the-man-who-challenged-putin/a-64744266, accessed: 20 July 2023; Andrei Kolesnikov, 'Is There a Future in Politics for Russia's Wagner Boss, Yevgeny Prigozhin?, In the current political system, Prigozhin can only be against the elite so long as he is for Putin. It would take the slightest sign from the president for the Wagner boss to disappear', Carnegie Endowment for International Peace, https://carnegieendowment.org/politika/89962, accessed: 20 July 2023; Isabel van Brugen, 'Putin's Kremlin Strongmen Warn Prigozhin Over Political Ambitions—ISW', *Newsweek*, 18 May 2023, https://www.newsweek.com/putin-siloviki-kremlin-strongmen-warn-prigozhin-political-ambitions-wagner-group-1801107, accessed: 20 July 2023; Aleksandr Simonov, 'Prigozhin zayavil o namerenii ballotirovat'sya v prezidenty v 2024 godu (VIDEO),' *Rusvesna*, 11 March 2023, https://rusvesna.su/news/1678536206, accessed: 20 March 2023.
8. Matvej Dubianskij, 'De-Nazification is an Absolute Must': Moscow's Narrative in Ukraine,' *Global Risk Insights*, 25 July 2022, https://globalriskinsights.com/2022/07/de-nazification-is-an-absolute-must-moscows-narrative-in-ukraine/, accessed: 7 August 2023.
9. 'Eks-analitik TSRU prognoziruyet porazheniye VSU uzhe cherez paru nedel', *Antifashist*, 11 July 2023, https://antifashist.com/item/eks-analitik-cru-prognoziruet-porazhenie-vsu-uzhe-cherez-paru-nedel.html, accessed: 11 July 2023.
10. Dmitriy Plotnikov, 'General SSHA: 'My by nikogda ne otpravili nashikh soldat v takoye nastupleniye', *Pravda*, 8 July 2023, https://military.pravda.ru/news/1854974-my_by_nikogda_ne_otpravili/, accessed: 8 July 2023.
11. Isabelle Khurshudyan: 'Ukraine's top general, Valery Zaluzhny, wants shells, planes and patience', *The Washington Post*, 30 June 2023, https://www.washingtonpost.com/world/2023/06/30/valery-zaluzhny-ukraine-general-interview/, accessed: 6 July 2023; 'Otkroveniya Zaluzhnogo': glavkom VSU nashel vinovnykh v problemakh kontrnastupa', *RIA*, 2 July 2023, https://ria.ru/20230702/zaluzhnyy-1881678702.html, accessed: 6 July 2023; Andrey Fedorov, Yuliya Leonova, Bogdan Stepovoy, 'Uboynaya taktika: VFU pytayutsya vzlomat' rossiyskuyu oboronu pekhotoy, Pochemu vooruzhennyye formirovaniya smenili taktiku i skol'ko mogut prodlit'sya ataki bez ispol'zovaniya bronetekhniki', *Izvestia*, 8 July 2023, https://iz.ru/1541093/andrei-fedorov-iuliia-leonova-bogdan-stepovoi/uboinaia-taktika-vfu-pytaiutsia-vzlomat-rossiiskuiu-oboronu-pekhotoi, accessed: 8 July 2023.
12. David Sacks, 'The Truth About Ukraine's Failing Counteroffensive And The Peace That Could Have Been,' *The Federalist*, 20 June 2023, https://thefederalist.com/2023/06/20/heres-the-truth-about-ukraines-failing-counteroffensive-and-the-peace-that-could-have-been/, accessed: 20 July 2023; 'Telegraph: Failure of AFU Counter-offensive Will Push Ukraine to Make Territorial Concessions, Telegraph columnist Robert Clark has said that Ukraine will have to make territorial concessions in the event of the final failure of the AFU counter-offensive,' *Global Euronews*, 19 July 2023, https://globaleuronews.com/2023/07/19/telegraph-failure-of-afu-counter-offensive-will-push-ukraine-to-make-territorial-concessions/, accessed: 20 July 2023; Vijainder K Thakur, 'Ukraine's Counter-Offensive Fails, Military Mauled; Russia's 'Super Weapon' Dents Kyiv's Plan: Analysis, Ukraine's much-touted counteroffensive appears to be tumbling largely due to the Russian military's excellent military tactics and cutting-edge weapons', *The EurAsian Times*, 28 June 2023, https://www.eurasiantimes.com/ukraines-counter-offensive-fails-military-mauled-russias/, accesssed: 20 July 2023; 'Ukrainskoye kontrnastuplenie idet medlenneye, chem ozhidal Pentagon', *Reuters, Rusvesna*, 8 July 2023, https://rusvesna.su/news/1688508139, accessed: 8 July 2023.
13. Brad Lendon, 'Putin can call up all the Troops he wants, but Russia can't train or support them', CNN, 22 September 2022; 'Russian "partial mobilisation" is a military gamble far from being won', *Le Monde*, 22 September 2022; 'Mobilization can't save Russia's War', *Foreign Policy*, 4 October 2022.
14. Sonam Sheth, John Haltiwanger, 'Putin tried to justify his war against Ukraine by calling for the 'de-Nazification' of a democratic country led by a Jewish president,' *Business Insider*, 24 February 2022, https://www.businessinsider.com/putin-tries-justifying-ukraine-war-denazification-zelensky-jewish-president-2022-2, accessed: 7 August 2023; Zoya Sheftalovich, 'Putin wants to de-Nazify Ukraine — that's ludicrous, say the country's Jews, Jewish Ukrainians give short shrift to Putin's claim he is out to save them from Nazis', *Politico*, 25 April 2022, https://www.politico.eu/article/in-the-face-of-war-ukraine-jews-embrace-a-dual-identity/, accessed: 7 August 2023.
15. Claire Gilbody-Dickerson, 'What does 'de-Nazification' mean? Putin's justification for Russia's Ukraine invasion debunked point by point, Vladimir Putin has invaded Ukraine saying he had to defend Russians from 'genocide' and 'de-Nazify' the country. Here we explain the difference between his claims and reality', *Inews.co.uk*, 24 February 2022, https://inews.co.uk/news/world/what-does-de-nazification-mean-putins-justification-for-russias-ukraine-invasion-debunked-point-by-point-1482361, accessed: 7 August 2023; Olivia B. Maxman, 'Historians on What Putin Gets Wrong About 'Denazification' in Ukraine', *Time*, https://time.com/6154493/denazification-putin-ukraine-history-context/, accessed: 7 August 2023.

16 Chuck Devore, 'Why Is Putin Talking About 'De-Nazifying' Ukraine?', *The Federalist*, 16 March 2022, https://thefederalist.com/2022/03/16/why-is-putin-talking-about-de-nazifying-ukraine/, accessed: 7 August 2023; 'Zack Beauchamp, Putin's 'Nazi' rhetoric reveals his terrifying war aims in Ukraine, Russia's president says he wants the 'de-Nazification' of Ukraine. That actually means regime change', *Vox*, 24 February 2022, https://www.vox.com/2022/2/24/22948944/putin-ukraine-nazi-russia-speech-declare-war, accessed: 7 August 2023.

17 Andrew Roth, 'Russia threatens Ukraine's 'decision-making centres' if Kyiv uses western arms in Crimea, Use of US- and UK-supplied missiles would mark west's 'full involvement', Russian defence minister says', *The Guardian,* 20 June 2023, https://www.theguardian.com/world/2023/jun/20/russia-threatens-ukraine-decision-making-centres-kyiv-western-arms-crimea, accessed: 7 August 2023; Frank Chung: 'Moscow threatens to strike 'decision-making centres' if Ukraine uses US rockets to hit Russia, Moscow says it will have 'no choice' but to strike at 'decision-making centres' outside of Ukraine if Kyiv uses American missiles against Russia', *News.com.au*, 4 June 2022, https://www.news.com.au/world/europe/moscow-threatens-to-strike-decisionmaking-centres-if-ukraine-uses-us-rockets-to-hit-russia/news-story/e5cfa6cbf7b74a8aa1e05bd2e05ef63e, accessed: 7 August 2023.

18 'Russia Strikes Ukrainian 'Decision-Making Center' – Ministry of Defense', *Infowars*, 17 June 2023, https://www.infowars.com/posts/russia-strikes-ukrainian-decision-making-center-ministry-of-defense/, accessed: 7 August 2023.

19 'V Minoborony RF prigrozili udarom po Kiyevu v sluchaye ataki rossiyskoy territorii', *Antifashist*, 26 April 2022, https://antifashist.com/item/v-minoborony-rf-prigrozili-udarom-po-kievu-v-sluchae-ataki-rossijskoj-territorii.html, accessed: 9 July 2023 & 'Mash: VSU popytalis' atakovat' AES v Smolenskoy oblasti i voyennyy aerodrom v Kaluzhskoy', *Pravda*, 9 July 2023, https://military.pravda.ru/news/1855159-ukraina_pytalas_atakovat_aes_v_smolenskoi_oblasti/, accessed: 9 July 2023.

20 'Bespilotnik upal v neskol'kikh kilometrakh ot Kurskoy AES, Vzorvavshiysya v Kurchatove bespilotnik upal v neskol'kikh kilometrakh ot Kurskoy AES', *RIA*, 14 July 2023, https://ria.ru/20230714/aes-1884132174.html, accessed: 14 July 2023; 'Ukraina pytalas' atakovat' Kurskuyu AES i voyennyy aerodrom pod Voronezhem', *Antifashist*, 14 July 2023, https://antifashist.com/item/ukraina-pytalas-atakovat-kurskuyu-aes-i-voennyj-aerodrom-pod-voronezhem.html, accessed: 14 July 2023; 'Kiyev prizval FRG ne delat' oshibok Merkel' i podderzhat' chlenstvo strany v NATO, Glava MID Ukrainy Kuleba: FRG ne nuzhno povtoryat' oshibk u Merkel' i podderzhat' vstupleniye Kiyeva v NATO', *Izvestia*, 10 July 2023, https://iz.ru/1542364/2023-07-10/kiev-prizval-frg-ne-delat-oshibok-merkel-i-podderzhat-chlenstvo-strany-v-nato, accessed: 10 July 2023.

21 Peter Dickinson, 'The 2008 Russo-Georgian War: Putin's green light', *The Atlantic Council*, 7 August 2021, https://www.atlanticcouncil.org/blogs/ukrainealert/the-2008-russo-georgian-war-putins-green-light/, accessed: 7 August 2023.

22 Bernd Riegert, 'Membership for Ukraine on agenda at NATO talks, The military alliance wants to assure Kyiv once again that it can join — one day, at least. Could a more concrete date emerge in Vilnius? Bernd Riegert looks at the questions facing NATO ahead of the summit', *Deutsche Welle*, 10 July 2023, https://www.dw.com/en/as-nato-meets-membership-for-ukraine-is-on-the-agenda/a-66162322, accessed: 20 July 2023; Dan Sabbagh, 'Zelenskiy fails in effort to secure invitation to join NATO at Vilnius summit, Leaders of military alliance sign off on declaration that does not give Ukraine firm membership timetable', *The Guardian*, 11 July 2023, https://www.theguardian.com/world/2023/jul/11/zelenskiy-accuses-nato-of-lack-of-respect-over-ukraine-membership, accessed: 20 July 2023; Sabine Siebold, John Irish and Andrew Gray, 'NATO welcomes Ukraine's membership but stops short of invitation', *Reuters*, 11 July 2023, https://www.reuters.com/world/nato-summit-seeks-agreement-ukraine-bid-after-turkey-deal-sweden-2023-07-10/, accessed: 20 July 2023; Peter Dickinson: 'NATO summit leaves Ukrainians frustrated', *Atlantic Council,* 11 July 2023, https://www.atlanticcouncil.org/blogs/ukrainealert/nato-summit-leaves-ukrainians-frustrated/, accessed: 20 July 2023; 'NATO chief says no timetable set for Ukraine's membership, Ukrainian President Volodymyr Zelenskyy blasted the organisation's failure to set a clear timetable as 'absurd'', *Euronews*, 12 July 2023, https://www.euronews.com/2023/07/11/zelenskyy-hits-out-at-natos-absurd-refusal-to-give-ukraine-a-timetable-for-membership, accessed: 20 July 2023; Nikakikh ustupok: 'Germaniya namerena blokirovat' skoroye vstupleniye Ukrainy v NATO', *Pravda*, 10 July 2023, https://www.pravda.ru/news/world/1855402-aljans/, accessed: 10 July 2023.

23 Charlie Bradley, 'Viktor Orban warns 'we could end up in World War 3' as Hungarian PM defies West, The Hungarian government has been reluctant to criticise Russia and Vladimir Putin for the invasion of Ukraine', *Express*, 31 March 2023, https://www.express.co.uk/news/world/1753496/viktor-orban-third-world-war-hungary-russia-ukraine, accessed: 6 August 2023; Fabio G. C. Carisio, 'Increasingly Lethal Military Aid to Ukraine from NATO Powers is 'Deeply Immoral'. Croatian President spoke like Hungarian PM Orban, 'Ukraine will never retake Crimea' Milanovic said', *Veterans Today*, 31 January 2023, https://www.veteranstoday.com/2023/01/31/increasingly-lethal-military-aid-to-ukraine-from-nato-powers-is-deeply-immoral-croatian-president-spoke-like-hungarian-pm-orban/, accessed: 6 August 2023.

24 'Stoltenberg, Ukraine's victory is the starting point to moving forward with NATO membership', *The Kyiv Independent,* 15 May 2023, https://kyivindependent.com/stoltenberg-ukrainian-victory-is-the-nato-accession-talks-after/, accessed: 7 August 2023; 'Stoltenberg: no point discussing how Ukraine can join NATO if it does not prevail in war first, NATO's secretary general has said he expects the alliance to agree a 'multi-year programme' to assist Ukraine in its desire to join the organisation, and that there was no 'meaning in discussing when and how Ukraine can become a member of the alliance' unless it prevails in the war 'as a sovereign independent nation in Europe', *The Guardian*, 15 May 2023, https://www.theguardian.com/world/live/2023/may/15/russia-ukraine-war-latest-g7-reportedly-set-to-tighten-russia-sanctions-france-to-send-kyiv-military-aid-live?filterKeyEvents=false&page=with:block-646208dd8f0822aea831dd26#block-646208dd8f0822aea831dd26, accessed: 7 August 2023; 'Stoltenberg Says Ukraine Joining NATO During War 'Not On The Agenda', *Radio Free Europe,* 24 May 2023, https://www.rferl.org/a/stoltenberg-ukraine-join-nato-war-agenda/32426056.html, accessed: 7 August 2023; 'Stoltenberg says NATO will invite Ukraine to join 'when conditions are met', *France24*, 11 July 2023, https://www.france24.com/en/europe/20230711-%F0%9F%94%B4-live-nato-wrestles-with-ukraine-bid-at-summit-on-russia-s-doorstep, accessed: 7 August 2023.

25 Jeremy Herb, 'CNN Exclusive: Biden says war with Russia must end before NATO can consider membership for Ukraine', *CNN*, 9 July 2023, https://edition.cnn.com/2023/07/09/politics/joe-biden-ukraine-nato-russia-cnntv/index.html, accessed: 7 August 2023; Lexie Schapitl, 'Ukraine can't join NATO yet. But Biden says Zelenskyy is OK with that', *NPR*, 12 July 2023, https://www.npr.org/2023/07/12/1187291581/biden-vilnius-ukraine-nato, accessed: 7 July 2023; 'Ukraine is not ready for NATO membership, says Joe Biden, President Biden, who will attend a NATO summit in Europe this week, said it was 'premature' to allow Ukraine to join the alliance as the war with Russia continues', *Livemint*, 10 July 2023, https://www.livemint.com/news/world/ukraine-is-not-ready-for-nato-membership-says-joe-biden-11688936774832.html, accessed: 7 August 2023.

26 Oleg Volodin, 'Razvedchik, u RF snova poyavilsya absolyutnyy povod dlya ob'yavleniya voyny, Ukrainskiye vlasti ofitsial'no podtverdili prichastnost' Nezalezhnoy ko vzryvu 'Severnykh potokov' i teraktu na Krymskom mostu. Eksperty nazyvayut eto 'absolyutnym povodom dlya ob'yavleniya voyny', *Pravda*, 9 July 2023, https://www.pravda.ru/politics/1855087-war2ukraine/, accessed: 9 July 2023; 'Pochemu Rossiya i Ukraina do sikh por ofitsial'no ne ob'yavili voynu?', *Antifashist*, 9 July 2023, https://antifashist.com/item/pochemu-rossiya-i-ukraina-do-sih-por-oficialno-ne-obyavili-vojnu.html, acccssed: 9 July 2023.

27 Brent Cooper, 'Why doesn't Russia destroy the bridges across the Dnipro River to worsen Ukraine's military logistics?', *Quora*, 8 July 2022, https://www.quora.com/Why-doesnt-Russia-destroy-the-bridges-across-the-Dnipro-River-to-worsen-Ukraines-military-logistics, accessed: 7 August 2023.

28 Dmitriy Plotnikov, 'Litovkin ob'yasnil, pochemu mosty i porty Ukrainy do sikh por tsely', *Pravda*, 8 July 2023, https://military.

29 pravda.ru/news/1854946-pochemu_mosty_i_porty_ukrainy/, accessed: 8 July 2023.
29 'In Kherson, all bridges across the Dnieper were destroyed', *IntelDrop*, 11 November 2022, https://www.theinteldrop.org/2022/11/11/in-kherson-all-bridges-across-the-dnieper-were-destroyed/, accessed: 7 August 2023.
30 Snejana Farberov, 'Russians 'highly vulnerable' after Ukrainian forces bomb 3 bridges', *New York Post*, 28 July 2023, https://nypost.com/2022/07/28/russians-highly-vulnerable-after-ukrainian-forces-bomb-3-bridges/, accessed: 7 August 2023; 'Ukraine hits key Dnieper River bridges, Kyiv said it hit the main supply route between Kherson and the south bank of the Dnieper overnight. Meanwhile, calls for access to the Zaporizhzhia nuclear plant have grown after recent shelling. DW has the latest', *Deutsche Welle*, 8 August 2022, https://www.dw.com/en/russia-ukraine-updates-ukraine-hits-bridges-in-russian-held-kherson/a-62744486, accessed: 7 August 2023; 'US rocket system enables Ukraine to strike key supply bridge in Russian controlled region', *ABC*, 27 July 2022, https://www.abc.net.au/news/2022-07-28/us-rocket-system-enables-ukraine-to-strike-key-supply-bridge/101276082, accessed: 7 August 2023.
31 Niha Masih, 'What to know about the grain deal that Russia just pulled out of', *The Washington Post*, 18 July 2023, https://www.washingtonpost.com/world/2023/07/18/russia-grain-deal-ukraine/, accessed: 7 August 2023.
32 'Blast injures 10 near grain silos at Turkish port', *Reuters*, 7 August 2023, https://www.reuters.com/world/middle-east/blast-injures-10-near-grain-silos-turkish-port-2023-08-07/, accessed: 10 August 2023.
33 'TURKEY- a powerful explosion has destroyed The Turkish Grain silos, A grain silos blast in Turkey's Derince Port has injured at least 12 people. According to initial evaluations, the blast occurred due to wheat dust compression', *Greek City Times*, 10 August 2023, https://greekcitytimes.com/2023/08/08/turkey-a-powerful-explosion-has-destroyed-the-turkish-grain-silos/, accessed: 10 August 2023.
34 Marc Santora, Ivan Nechepurenko and Matthew Mpoke Bigg, 'Russia Bombards Ukraine Port After Bridge Attack and Grain Deal Collapse, Russian forces launched a barrage of missiles and drones at Odesa, not usually a major target, a day after important shifts in the conduct of the war', *The New York Times*, 18 July 2023, https://www.nytimes.com/2023/07/18/world/europe/russia-barrage-odesa-grain-bridge.html, accessed: 7 August 2023.
35 'Germaniya otkazalas' stroit' v Pol'she tsentr po remontu tankov, Germaniya otkazalas' ot idei stroitel'stva v Pol'she tsentra po remontu peredannykh Ukraine tankov Leopard, utverzhdayet gazeta Handelsblatt so ssylkoy na istochniki', *Rusvesna*, 12 July 2023, https://rusvesna.su/news/1689163134, accessed: 12 July 2023.
36 'Ukraine's Zelenskyy brings home Azovstal commanders from Turkey, Russia denounces the soldiers' return, accusing Kyiv and Ankara of violating a prisoner exchange deal under which the men were to remain in Turkey until the end of the war', *Aljazeera*, 8 July 2023, https://www.aljazeera.com/news/2023/7/8/ukraines-zelenskyy-returns-azov-commanders-released-to-turkey, accessed: 21 July 2023; Isabella Ramirez, 'Putin Cheated by Erdogan Right After Announcing Turkey Trip, The Kremlin accused Istanbul of betraying a prisoner agreement just as Vladimir Putin announced he will be making a rare overseas trip to visit his pal, President Erdoğan', *The Daily Beast*, 8 July 2023, https://www.thedailybeast.com/kremlins-not-happy-zelensky-brought-azov-commanders-home-from-turkey, accessed: 21 July 2023; 'Na Ukrainu iz Turtsii vozvrashcheny byvshiye v plenu komandiry natsbata 'Azov' (VIDEO)', *Rusvesna*, 8 July 2023, https://rusvesna.su/news/1688826426, accessed: 8 July 2023.
37 'Azov commanders return home: A diplomatic win for Ukraine, a slap in the face for Russia, When Ukraine's President Volodymyr Zelensky returned from a visit to Turkey last weekend, he did not board the plane alone. Joining him were five former Azov commanders, captured by Russia in the 2022 siege of Mariupol and later handed over to Turkey in a prisoner exchange. Their return to Ukraine was a major diplomatic win for Ukraine and a slap in the face for Russia, who has since accused Turkey of violating the terms of the deal to score points with the West', *France24*, 12 July 2023, https://www.france24.com/en/europe/20230712-azov-commanders-return-home-a-diplomatic-win-for-ukraine-a-slap-in-the-face-for-russia, accessed: 21 July 2023; Dmitriy Plotnikov: 'Na Ukrainu iz Turtsii vozvrashcheny sdavshiyesya v Mariupole komandiry natsbata 'Azov'*, * - priznan resheniyem Verkhovnogo Suda Rossiyskoy Federatsii ot 02.08.2022 terroristicheskoy organizatsiyey, yego deyatel'nost' zapreshchena na territorii RF', *Pravda*, 8 July 2023, https://military.pravda.ru/news/1855009-byvshie_v_plenu_komandiry_nacbata/, accessed: 8 July 2023; 'Turtsiya narushila dogovoronnosti, peredav komandirov 'Azova' Kiyevu — Peskov', *Antifashist*, 8 July 2023, https://antifashist.com/item/turciya-narushila-dogovorennosti-peredav-komandirov-azova-kievu-peskov.html, accessed: 8 July 2023; Lyubov' Stepushova: 'Khitryy Erdogan otpravil na vernuyu smert' boyevikov Azova*, Narushiv dogovorennosti s RF ob uderzhivanii boyevikov ' Azova'* v Turtsii, prezident Redzhep Erdogan podpisal im smertnyy prigovor. No obespechil Turtsii loyal'nost' Zapada. * - priznan resheniyem Verkhovnogo Suda Rossiyskoy Federatsii ot 02.08.2022 terroristicheskoy organizatsiyey, yego deyatel'nost' zapreshchena na territorii RF', *Pravda*, 9 July 2023, https://www.pravda.ru/world/1855101-azov_erdogan/ accessed: 9 July 2023.
38 'Satanovskiy: plennykh natsistov i 'azovtsev'* bol'she byt' ne dolzhno, * - priznan resheniyem Verkhovnogo Suda Rossiyskoy Federatsii ot 02.08.2022 terroristicheskoy organizatsiyey, yego deyatel'nost' zapreshchena na territorii RF', *Pravda*, 11 July 2023, https://military.pravda.ru/news/1855786-plennykh_azovcev_bolshe/ accessed: 11 July 2023.
39 Josh Pennington, Alex Stambaugh, Brad Lendon, Christian Edwards, 'Ukraine claims responsibility for new attack on key Crimea bridge', *CNN*, 17 July 2023, https://edition.cnn.com/2023/07/16/europe/russia-crimea-bridge-intl-hnk/index.html accessed: 10 August 2023.
40 Christina Lu, 'Putin Seeks Revenge After Kerch Bridge Explosion, The blast dealt a strategic blow a day after the Russian leader's birthday. Now, he's retaliating', *Foreign Policy*, 10 October 2022, https://foreignpolicy.com/2022/10/10/russia-ukraine-bridge-explosion-putin-war-revenge-attack/ accessed: 10 August 2023; Ian Collier, 'Vladimir Putin says missile strikes across Ukraine are in retaliation for Crimea bridge 'terrorist' blast, The Russian president says Monday's missile strikes were in retaliation for an attack on the Kerch Bridge that links Russia to the annexed Crimean peninsula which was a 'terrorist act'', *Sky News*, 10 October 2022, https://news.sky.com/story/putin-says-missile-strikes-across-ukraine-retaliation-for-crimea-bridge-blast-12717302 accessed: 10 August 2023; Isobel Koshiw: 'Russia carries out more mass strikes on Ukraine's energy infrastructure, Power outages reported after barrage of rockets fired at several regions in second such attack in days', *The Guardian*, 16 December 2022, https://www.theguardian.com/world/2022/dec/16/russia-begins-mass-air-strike-in-apparent-move-to-destroy-ukraines-power-grid accessed: 10 August 2023.
41 Julian E. Barnes, Adam Entous, Eric Schmitt, Anton Troianovski, 'Ukrainians Were Likely Behind Kremlin Drone Attack, U.S. Officials Say, American spy agencies do not know exactly who carried out the attack this month, but suggest it was part of a series of covert operations orchestrated by Ukraine's security services', *The New York Times*, 24 May 2023, https://www.nytimes.com/2023/05/24/us/politics/ukraine-kremlin-drone-attack.html accessed: 10 August 2023; Pjotr Sauer, Dan Sabbagh, 'Kremlin drone incident: Zelenskiy denies Russian claim Ukraine attempted to kill Putin, Ukraine president denies involvement, saying 'we fight on our territory and defend our towns and cities' after Kremlin blames Kyiv', *The Guardian*, 4 May 2023, https://www.theguardian.com/world/2023/may/03/russia-accuses-ukraine-of-trying-to-kill-vladimir-putin-with-kremlin-drone-strike accessed: 10 August 2023; Josh Pennington, Simone McCarthy, Sophie Jeong, Christian Edwards, 'Ukraine carried out drone attack on Moscow, officials say', *CNN*, 24 July 2023, https://edition.cnn.com/2023/07/23/europe/ukraine-russia-drone-attacks-hit-moscow-intl-hnk/index.html accessed: 10 August 2023.
42 'Zelenskiy smenil komanduyushchego Natsgvardiyey. Teper' vsya Natsgvardiya stanet 'Azovom', *Antifashist*, 9 July 2023, https://antifashist.com/item/zelenskij-smenil-komanduyushhego-nacgvardiej-teper-vsya-nacgvardiya-stanet-azovom.html accessed: 9 July 2023.
43 'Profile: Who are Ukraine's far-right Azov regiment?, The far-right neo-Nazi group has expanded to become part of Ukraine's armed forces, a street militia and a political party'. *Aljazeera*, 1 March 2023, https://www.aljazeera.com/news/2022/3/1/who-are-

the-azov-regiment accessed: 27 June 2023 & Fredrick Kunkle, Serhii Korolchuk, 'Ukraine's volunteer 'Kraken' unit takes the fight to the Russians', *The Washington Post*, 3 June, 2022, https://www.washingtonpost.com/world/2022/06/03/ukraine-kraken-volunteer-military-unit/ accessed: 27 June 2023; 'V MO RF soobshchili o porazhenii rayona sosredotocheniya rezervov natsbatal'ona 'Kraken' v DNR, Nachal'nik press-tsentra gruppirovki 'Yug' Vadim Astaf'yev rasskazal, chto aviatsiya nanesla raketno-bombovyye udary po ukrainskim voyennym i opornym punktam VSU na soledaro-artemovskom i aleksandro-kalinovskom napravleniyakh', *TASS*, 8 July 2023, https://tass.ru/armiya-i-opk/18223101 accessed: 8 July 2023.

44 Fredrick Kunkle, Serhii Korolchuk, 'Ukraine's volunteer 'Kraken' unit…'.

45 Alan Ripp, 'Ukraine's Nazi problem is real, even if Putin's 'denazification' claim isn't, Not acknowledging this threat means that little is being done to guard against it', *CNBC*, 5 March, 2022, https://www.nbcnews.com/think/opinion/ukraine-has-nazi-problem-vladimir-putin-s-denazification-claim-war-ncna1290946 accessed: 10 August 2023; Claire Gilbody-Dickerson, 'What does 'de-Nazification' mean? Putin's justification for Russia's Ukraine invasion debunked point by point, Vladimir Putin has invaded Ukraine saying he had to defend Russians from 'genocide' and 'de-Nazify' the country. Here we explain the difference between his claims and reality', Inews.co.uk, 24 February 2022, https://inews.co.uk/news/world/what-does-de-nazification-mean-putins-justification-for-russias-ukraine-invasion-debunked-point-by-point-1482361 accessed: 7 August 2023; Olivia B. Maxman, 'Historians on What Putin Gets Wrong About 'Denazification' in Ukraine', *Time*, https://time.com/6154493/denazification-putin-ukraine-history-context/ accessed: 7 August 2023.

46 Fredrick Kunkle, Serhii Korolchuk, 'Ukraine's volunteer 'Kraken' unit takes the fight to the Russians', *The Washington Post*, 3 June, 2022, https://www.washingtonpost.com/world/2022/06/03/ukraine-kraken-volunteer-military-unit/ accessed: 27 June 2023.

47 Josh Cohen, 'Commentary: Ukraine's neo-Nazi problem', *Reuters*, 19 March 2018, https://www.reuters.com/article/us-cohen-ukraine-commentary-idUSKBN1GV2TY accessed: 11 August 2023.

48 Fredrick Kunkle, Serhii Korolchuk, 'Ukraine's volunteer 'Kraken' unit takes the fight to the Russians', *The Washington Post*, 3 June, 2022, https://www.washingtonpost.com/world/2022/06/03/ukraine-kraken-volunteer-military-unit/ accessed: 27 June 2023.

49 Fredrick Kunkle, Serhii Korolchuk, 'Ukraine's volunteer 'Kraken' unit takes the fight to the Russians', *The Washington Post*, 3 June, 2022, https://www.washingtonpost.com/world/2022/06/03/ukraine-kraken-volunteer-military-unit/ accessed: 27 June 2023.

50 Tara John, Tim Lister, 'A far-right battalion has a key role in Ukraine's resistance. Its neo-Nazi history has been exploited by Putin', *CNN*, 30 March 2022, https://edition.cnn.com/2022/03/29/europe/ukraine-azov-movement-far-right-intl-cmd/index.html accessed: 11 August 2023.

Chapter 2

1 Unless stated otherwise, based on cross-examination of contemporary reporting by contacts in Ukraine and Russia to Tom Cooper (and resulting reporting on Sarcastosaurus Blog, substack.com/@xxtomcooperxx), with details on the Wagner Group's casualties as provided by Mediazona, 'The Price of Bakhmut', en.zona.media, 10 June 2024, on basis of captured Russian documentation.

2 For a detailed reconstruction of the Battle of Popasna (including operations by the 24th Mechanised Brigade in reaction to assaults by Wagner PMC, and the death of one of Wagner-contracted Su-25-pilots, see Cooper et all, *War in Ukraine, Vol. 7*, pp.43-45.

3 For a detailed reconstruction of Russian attempts to achieve an operational-level breakthrough south and south-west of Lysychansk after securing Popasna, see Cooper et all, *War in Ukraine, Vol. 7*, pp.50 51.

4 For Ukrainian ballistic missile strikes on the Wagner HQ in Kadiivka, see, 'Russian Forces intercepted 4 Tochka-U Missiles launched by Ukrainian Armed Forces', *Global Defence News*, 10 June 2022 & 'Ukrainian Troops destroyed Russian barracks in occupied Kadiivka, Luhansk Oblast', *Euromaidan Press*, 26 July 2022.

5 Cooper et all, *War in Ukraine*, Vol.7, pp.13-14.

6 Filip Lebedev and Felix Light, 'Wagner's Convicts tell of Horrors of Ukraine War and Loyalty to their Leader', Reuters, 16 March 2023; 'Russian Prisoners face grim Fate in Ukraine War with Wagner Group', EssaNews, 10 June 2024; 'The Price of Bakhmut' (in Ukrainian), *Mediazona*, 10 June 2024.

7 For a reconstruction on the battle for Soledar in late December 2022 and early January 2023, see Tom Cooper, 'Ukraine War, 10 January 2023', 'Ukraine War, 13 January 2023', and 'Ukraine War, 15 January 2023', *Sarcastosaurus Blog*, 10, 13, and 15 January 2023.

8 Tom Cooper 'Ukraine War, 13 January 2023', *Sarcastosaurus Blog*, 13 January 2023 & Tom Cooper, 'Ukraine War, 15 January 2023', *Sarcastosaurus Blog*, 15 January 2023.

9 According to Prigozhin's online statement, released in Russian social media on 17 February 2023, amongst those killed were four mercenaries from Finland that went missing during the Battle of Bakhmut.

Chapter 3

1 'Teper' u 'Vagnera' tri znakovykh pobedy — Popasnaya, Soledar i Artomovsk', *Rusvesna*, 21 May 2023, https://rusvesna.su/news/1684593557 accessed: 26 June 2023.

2 Benoît Vitkine, 'The political ambitions of Russia's Wagner Group boss, Yevgeny Prigozhin – known for his 'troll factories' responsible for electoral interference – is preparing to launch a conservative movement', *Le Monde*, 18 November 2022, https://www.lemonde.fr/en/international/article/2022/11/18/the-political-ambitions-of-russia-s-wagner-group-boss_6004751_4.html accessed: 20 July 2023; Maria Katarmadze, 'Who is Yevgeny Prigozhin, the man who challenged Putin?, The owner of the Wagner private military contractor and leader of a massive internet troll farm called for an armed rebellion to oust Russia's defense minister. But is he a threat to President Vladimir Putin?' *Deutsche Welle*, 25 June 2023, https://www.dw.com/en/who-is-yevgeny-prigozhin-the-man-who-challenged-putin/a-64744266 accessed: 20 July 2023; Andrei Kolesnikov, Is There a Future in Politics for Russia's Wagner Boss, Yevgeny Prigozhin?, In the current political system, Prigozhin can only be against the elite so long as he is for Putin. It would take the slightest sign from the president for the Wagner boss to disappear, Carnegie Endowment for International Peace, https://carnegieendowment.org/politika/89962 accessed: 20 July 2023; Isabel van Brugen, 'Putin's Kremlin Strongmen Warn Prigozhin Over Political Ambitions—ISW', *Newsweek*, 18 May 2023, https://www.newsweek.com/putin-siloviki-kremlin-strongmen-warn-prigozhin-political-ambitions-wagner-group-1801107 accessed: 20 July 2023; Aleksandr Simonov, 'Prigozhin zayavil o namerenii ballotirovat'sya v prezidenty v 2024 godu (VIDEO)', *Rusvesna*, 11 March 2023, https://rusvesna.su/news/1678536206 accessed: 12 March 2023.

3 'Yevgeniy Prigozhin rasskazal o situatsii v Artomovske i snabzhenii boyepripasami', *Antifashist*, 9 May 2023, https://antifashist.com/item/evgenij-prigozhin-rasskazal-o-situacii-v-artyomovske-i-snabzhenii-boepripasami.html, accessed: 26 June 2023.

4 'Yevgeniy Prigozhin rasskazal o situatsii v Artomovske i snabzhenii boyepripasami', *Antifashist*, 9 May 2023, https://antifashist.com/item/evgenij-prigozhin-rasskazal-o-situacii-v-artyomovske-i-snabzhenii-boepripasami.html, accessed: 26 June 2023.

5 Lyubov' Stepushova, 'Poslesloviye k obrashcheniyu Putina 26 iyunya: kadrovyye perestanovki neobkhodimy', *Pravda*, 27 June 2023, https://www.pravda.ru/politics/1851431-putin_wagner/, accessed: 27 June 2023.

6 Lyubov' Stepushova, 'Poslesloviye k obrashcheniyu Putina 26 iyunya: kadrovyye perestanovki neobkhodimy', *Pravda*, 27 June 2023, https://www.pravda.ru/politics/1851431-putin_wagner/, accessed: 27 June 2023.

7 'Surovikin, poyezd tronulsya', *Antifashist*, 8 May 2023, https://antifashist.com/item/surovikin-poezd-tronulsya.html, accessed: 26 June 2023.

8 'Teper' u 'Vagnera' tri znakovykh pobedy — Popasnaya, Soledar i Artomovsk', *Rusvesna*, 21 May 2023, https://rusvesna.su/news/1684593557, accessed: 27 June 2023.

9 Yaroslav Trofimov, 'Russia's Wagner Troops Exhaust Ukrainian Forces in Bakhmut, Deadly fight against the penal battalions threatens Kyiv's ability to mount spring offensive', *The Wall Street*

10 'WSJ: VSU nesut bol'shiye poteri na fronte Artomovsk-Soledar, bystro istoshchaya sily brigad,' *Rusvena,* https://rusvesna.su/news/1673440985, accessed: 27 June 2023.

Journal, 5 March 2023, https://www.wsj.com/articles/russias-wagner-troops-exhaust-ukrainian-forces-in-bakhmut-b58e726c, accessed: 27 'June 2023; Ne pora li VSU otstupit' ot Artomovska? — WSJ (FOTO)', *Rusvesna*, 12 January 2023, https://rusvesna.su/news/1673512361, accessed: 27 June 2023.

11 María R. Sahuquillo, Bakhmut, 'The fortress city at the center of bloodiest battle in Russia's war in Ukraine, Artillery bombardments and Wagner Group mercenaries have besieged the strategic town where the civilian population has been reduced to 10% of pre-war levels and fighting has been likened to WWI', *El Pais*, 23 December 2022, https://english.elpais.com/international/2022-12-23/bakhmut-the-fortress-city-at-the-center-of-bloodiest-battle-in-russias-war-in-ukraine.html, accessed: 27 June 2023; 'Bitva za Artomovsk — samaya krovavaya bitva za ves' konflikt', *El Pais, Rusvesna*, 16 January 2023, https://rusvesna.su/news/1673880136, accessed: 27 June 2023.

12 María R. Sahuquillo, María R. Sahuquillo, Bakhmut, 'The fortress city at the center of bloodiest battle in Russia's war in Ukraine, Artillery bombardments and Wagner Group mercenaries have besieged the strategic town where the civilian population has been reduced to 10% of pre-war levels and fighting has been likened to WWI', *El Pais*, 23 December 2022, https://english.elpais.com/international/2022-12-23/bakhmut-the-fortress-city-at-the-center-of-bloodiest-battle-in-russias-war-in-ukraine.html, accessed: 27 June 2023.

13 'Zelenskiy nazval sdachu Artomovska velichayshim porazheniyem Ameriki posle V'yetnama', *Pravda*, 9 April 2023, https://military.pravda.ru/news/1820279-zelenskii_nazval_sdachu_artemovska/ accessed: 27 June 2023.

14 'Prigozhin vystupil vpervyye posle okonchaniya 'myatezha'. On rasskazal, kak eto proizoshlo i kakiye byli tseli, Press-sluzhba osnovatelya CHVK 'Vagner' Yevgeniya Prigozhina 26 iyunya opublikovala pervoye audiosoobshcheniye ot yego imeni s vechera 24 iyunya, kogda kolonny 'vagnerovtsev' prekratili svoy 'marsh spravedlivosti' v storonu Moskvy', *RTVI*, 26 June 2023, https://rtvi.com/news/prigozhin-vystupil-vpervye-posle-okonchaniya-myatezha-on-rasskazal-kak-eto-proizoshlo-i-kakie-byli-czeli/?utm_source=smi2, accessed: 28 June 2023.

15 'What happened when Russia's air force attacked Wagner's rebels?, The mercenaries' downing of several aircraft is another embarrassment for Moscow', *The Economist*, https://www.economist.com/the-economist-explains/2023/06/27/what-happened-when-russias-air-force-attacked-wagners-rebels, accessed: 10 August 2023.

16 'Wagner's feud with Russian army escalates amid reports of not-so-friendly fire, The feud between Yevgeny Prigozhin and the Kremlin's military leaders appears to be boiling over again', *Politico*, 5 June 2023, https://www.politico.eu/article/russia-soldiers-friendly-fire-wagner-group-yevgeny-prigozhin-bakhmut-ukraine-war/, accessed: 10 August 2023.

17 Patrick Reevell, 'Wagner mercenary chief calls for armed rebellion against Russian military leadership, The FSB called on Wagner fighters not to follow Prigozhin's orders', *ABC News*, 24 June 2023, https://abcnews.go.com/International/wagner-mercenary-chief-calls-armed-rebellion-russian-military/story?id=100335756, accessed: 10 August 2023.

18 'V Belorussii podgotovili palatochnyy lager' dlya CHVK 'Vagner'. Chto seychas proiskhodit s kompaniyey', *Antifashist*, 1 July 2023, https://antifashist.com/item/v-belorussii-podgotovili-palatochnyj-lager-dlya-chvk-vagner-chto-sejchas-proishodit-s-kompaniej.html, accessed: 1 July 2023.

19 Address to citizens of Russia (by Russian president Vladimir Putin), Kremlin, 24 June 2023, http://en.kremlin.ru/events/president/news/71496, accessed: 27 June 2023.

20 Pepe Escobar, 'A Matryoshka of Psyops: And Why General Armageddon Is Not Going Anywhere', *Strategic Culture*, 30 June 2023, https://strategic-culture.org/news/2023/06/30/a-matryoshka-of-psyops-and-why-general-armageddon-is-not-going-anywhere/, accessed: 30 June 2023.

21 'Sergey Surovikin calls on Wagner PMC to resolve problems peacefully, not to aid enemy, Russia's Deputy Commander of Russian joint forces in the special military operation area added that he arrived from the front line under order of the Defense Ministry board', *TASS*, 24 June 2023, https://tass.com/russia/1637469, accessed: 29 June 2023.

22 'Vas obmanom vtyanuli v prestupnuyu avantyuru Prigozhina'. Ministerstvo oborony RF obratilos' k boytsam CHVK 'Vagner', *Antifashist*, 24 June 2023, https://antifashist.com/item/vas-obmanom-vtyanuli-v-prestupnuyu-avantyuru-prigozhina-ministerstvo-oborony-rf-obratilos-k-bojcam-chvk-vagner.html, accessed: 29 June 2023.

23 'Vas obmanom vtyanuli v prestupnuyu avantyuru Prigozhina'. Ministerstvo oborony RF obratilos' k boytsam CHVK 'Vagner', *Antifashist*, 24 June 2023, https://antifashist.com/item/vas-obmanom-vtyanuli-v-prestupnuyu-avantyuru-prigozhina-ministerstvo-oborony-rf-obratilos-k-bojcam-chvk-vagner.html, accessed: 29 June 2023.

24 Address to citizens of Russia (by Russian president Vladimir Putin), Kremlin, 26 June 2023, http://en.kremlin.ru/events/president/transcripts/71528, accessed: 27 June 2023.

25 'Prigozhin vystupil vpervyye posle okonchaniya 'myatezha'. On rasskazal, kak eto proizoshlo i kakiye byli tseli, Press-sluzhba osnovatelya CHVK 'Vagner' Yevgeniya Prigozhina 26 iyunya opublikovala pervoye audiosoobshcheniye ot yego imeni s vechera 24 iyunya, kogda kolonny 'vagnerovtsev' prekratili svoy 'marsh spravedlivosti' v storonu Moskvy', *RTVI*, 26 June 2023, https://rtvi.com/news/prigozhin-vystupil-vpervye-posle-okonchaniya-myatezha-on-rasskazal-kak-eto-proizoshlo-i-kakie-byli-czeli/?utm_source=smi2, accessed: 28 June 2023; Vasco Cotovio, Katharina Krebs, Gianluca Mezzofiore, Paul P. Murphy, Allegra Goodwin: 'Wagner's Prigozhin apparently seen in public for first time since failed mutiny', *CNN*, 19 July 2023, https://edition.cnn.com/2023/07/19/europe/prigozhin-wagner-belarus-appears-intl/index.html, accessed: 21 July 2023.

26 Nikita Shmelov, 'Myatezh, 'Marsh spravedlivosti', 'I vnov' prodolzhayetsya boy!' A budut li vyvody?, ' *Antifashist*, 5 July 2023, https://antifashist.com/item/myatezh-marsh-spravedlivosti-i-vnov-prodolzhaetsya-boj-a-budut-li-vyvody.html, accessed: 8 July 2023.

27 'Prigozhin zayavil o vozvrashchenii CHVK 'Vagner' na polya srazheniy v blizhaysheye vremya', *Antifashist*, 3 July 2023, https://antifashist.com/item/prigozhin-zayavil-o-vozvrashhenii-chvk-vagner-na-polya-srazhenij-v-blizhajshee-vremya.html accessed: 8 July 2023.

28 Mary Ilyusina, Robin Dixon, Natalia Abbakumova, 'Putin met with Wagner chief Prigozhin after mutiny, Kremlin says', *The Washington Post*, 10 July 2023, https://www.washingtonpost.com/world/2023/07/10/russia-wagner-putin-prigozhin-meeting/, accessed: 21 July 2023; Isabel van Brugen, 'Putin's Meeting With Prigozhin After Mutiny Raises Questions', *Newsweek*, 10 July 2023, https://www.newsweek.com/putin-meeting-prigozhin-kremlin-after-mutiny-wagner-group-peskov-1811907, accessed: 21 July 2023; Will Stewart, 'Putin holds secret meeting with Yevgeny Prigozhin amid claims the Wagner chief will be tasked with assassinating Zelensky as he seeks to return to favour in Moscow, A three-hour meeting between Putin and Prigozhin took place at the Kremlin, Prigozhin may target Zelensky to work his way back in with Putin, some claim', *The Daily Mail*, 10 July 2023, https://www.dailymail.co.uk/news/article-12282027/Putin-holds-meeting-Yevgeny-Prigozhin-amid-claims-Wagner-chief-target-Zelensky.html, accessed: 21 July 2023; Henry Astier, 'Wagner boss Yevgeny Prigozhin met Russia's Vladimir Putin after mutiny', *BBC*, 10 July 2023, https://www.bbc.com/news/world-europe-66154909, accessed: 21 July 2023; 'Putin vstrechalsya s Prigozhinym i boytsami CHVK 'Vagner' v Kremle, Cherez pyat' dney posle popytki 'myatezha' sostoyalas' vstrecha prezidenta Rossii Vladimira Putina i rukovodstva CHVK 'Vagner'v Kremle. Na peregovory pribyli 35 chelovek: komandiry otryadov, predstaviteli kompanii i Yevgeniy Prigozhin. Ob etom soobshchil press-sekretar' glavy gosudarstva Dmitriy Peskov', *Pravda*, 10 July 2023, https://www.pravda.ru/news/politics/1855347-vladimir_putin_evgenii_prigozhin/, accessed: 12 July 2023; 'Lyubov' Aleksandrovna Stepushova, Kiyevu naneson udar pered sammitom NATO: Putin ostavil CHVK 'Vagner' v SVO', *Pravda*, 10 July 2023, https://military.pravda.ru/1855394-putin_wagner/, accessed: 12 July 2023.

29 'Prigozhin nuzhen Putinu, a Putin Prigozhinu', *Antifashist,* 11 July 2023, https://antifashist.com/item/prigozhin-nuzhen-putinu-a-putin-prigozhinu.html, accessed: 12 July 2023.

30 Ellen Joanes, 'Wagner's real money never came from diamonds and gold, Wagner's businesses in Africa isolate and create dependent economies, not funding for private armies', *Vox*, 2 July 2023, https://www.vox.com/world-politics/2023/7/2/23781794/wagner-group-africa-russia-uae-putin, accessed: 10 August 2023; Andrew Ross Sorokin, Ravi Mattu, Bernhad Warner, Sarah Kessler, Michael J. de la Merced, Lauren Hirsch, Ephrat Livni, 'Inside Yevgeny Prigozhin's Money-Making Machine, The man who led a rebellion against President Vladimir Putin built a multinational commercial enterprise that helped fund his military operations', *The New York Times*, 26 June 2023, https://www.nytimes.com/2023/06/26/business/dealbook/prigozhins-wagner-money.html, accessed: 10 August 2023.

31 'Vagner' polnost'yu obespechivalsya gosudarstvom, za god CHVK poluchila boleye 86 mlrd rubley, — Putin (VIDEO)', *Rusvesna*, 27 June 2023, https://rusvesna.su/news/1687868386, accessed: 27 June 2023.

32 As of 10 August 2023.

33 Meeting with Defence Ministry personnel, The President met in the Kremlin with military personnel of the Defence Ministry, The Kremlin, Moscow, 27 June 2023, http://en.kremlin.ru/events/president/news/71535, accessed: 28 June 2023; 'Putin zayavil, chto CHVK 'Vagner' polnost'yu obespechivalas' gosudarstvom, Putin: 'Vagner' finansirovalo gosudarstvo, za god CHVK poluchila boleye 86 milliardov rubley', *RIA*, 27 June 2023, https://ria.ru/20230627/vagner-1880724094.html, accessed: 27 June 2023.

34 'Prigozhin rasskazal, chto CHVK 'Vagner' na samom dele ne CHVK', *Federal Press*, 5 June 2023, https://fedpress.ru/news/52/society/3246455?utm_source=24smi&utm_medium=referral&utm_term=10949&utm_content=5083926&utm_campaign=1630&utm_referrer=24smi.info, accessed: 27 June 2023.

35 'Wagner cost Russia Suspiciously Little Money', *Bloomberg*, 4 July 2023, https://www.bloomberg.com/opinion/articles/2023-07-04/financing-wagner-group-cost-russia-surprisingly-little-money#xj4y7vzkg, accessed: 10 August 2023; 'Vagner' po goskontraktam poluchil 858 milliardov rubley, Televedushchiy Kiselev: CHVK 'Vagner' Prigozhina poluchila po goskontraktam 858 mlrd rubley', *RIA*, 2 July 2023, https://ria.ru/20230702/vagner-1881731788.html, accessed: 8 July 2023.

36 'Military: Wagner Group comparable to armies of Hungary, Slovakia in size', *The Kyiv Independent*, 2 April 2023, https://kyivindependent.com/military-wagner-group-boasts-army-size-equal-to-hungary-slovakia/, accessed: 10 August 2023.

37 'Skol'ko tekhniki 'Vagnera' shlo na Moskvu: khronologiya sobytiy (VIDEO)', *Rusvesna*, 25 June 2023, https://rusvesna.su/news/1687684915, accessed: 27 June 2023.

38 'Skol'ko tekhniki 'Vagnera' shlo na Moskvu: khronologiya sobytiy (VIDEO)', *Rusvesna*, 25 June 2023, https://rusvesna.su/news/1687684915, accessed: 27 June 2023.

39 'CHVK 'Vagner' peredast tyazholuyu voyennuyu tekhniku Armii Rossii, — Minoborony', *Rusvesna*, 27 June 2023, https://rusvesna.su/news/1687853903, accessed: 27 June 2023; 'Lukashenko prizval ne boyat'sya boytsov CHVK 'Vagner'', *Antifashist*, 27 June 2023, https://antifashist.com/item/lukashenko-prizval-ne-boyatsya-bojcov-chvk-vagner.html, accessed: 27 June 2023.

40 'Putin reinforces his 'personal guard' with tanks and artillery', *Time News*, 29 June 2023, https://time.news/putin-reinforces-his-personal-guard-with-tanks-and-artillery/, accessed: 21 July 2023; 'After Wagner? How The Russian National Guard Could Become Putin's True 'Personal Army', A bill introduced to the Russian State Duma this week would allow the National Guard of Russia to receive tanks and other heavy military equipment and could turn the structure directly under Putin's command into a second army', *World Crunch*, 19 July 2023, https://worldcrunch.com/focus/russian-national-guard-putin, accessed: 21 July 2023; 'U Rosgvardii poyavyatsya tanki i tyazheloye vooruzheniye – Zolotov', *Antifashist*, 27 June 2023, https://antifashist.com/item/u-rosgvardii-poyavyatsya-tanki-i-tyazheloe-vooruzhenie-zolotov.html, accessed: 27 June 2023.

41 'Vooruzhennymi Silami Rossiyskoy Federatsii v sootvetstvii s planom zavershayetsya priyem vooruzheniya i voyennoy tekhniki ot podrazdeleniy gruppy 'Vagner'', the Ministry of Defence of the Russian Federation, 12 July 2023, https://t.me/mod_russia/28295 accessed: 12 July 2023; 'CHVK 'Vagner' peredala VS RF vooruzheniye i tekhniku', *Antifashist*, 12 July 2023, https://antifashist.com/item/chvk-vagner-peredala-vs-rf-vooruzhenie-i-tehniku.html accessed: 12 July 2023; Bogdan Stepovoy, Andrey Fedorov, Yuliya Leonova, 'Vstrechay oruzhiye: armiya prinyala u gruppy 'Vagner' 2 tys. yedinits tekhniki, Uspekhi VS RF vozle sela Torskoye sozdayut usloviya dlya ryvka na Krasnyy Liman i Izyum, polagayut eksperty', *Izvestia*, 13 July 2023, https://iz.ru/1543362/bogdan-stepovoi-andrei-fedorov-iuliia-leonova/vstrechai-oruzhie-armiia-priniala-u-gruppy-vagner-2-tys-edinitc-tekhniki, accessed: 13 July 2023.

42 'Vooruzhennymi Silami Rossiyskoy Federatsii v sootvetstvii s planom zavershayetsya priyem vooruzheniya i voyennoy tekhniki ot podrazdeleniy gruppy 'Vagner'', the Ministry of Defence of the Russian Federation, 12 July 2023, https://t.me/mod_russia/28295, accessed: 12 July 2023.

43 'Prigozhin in video tells Wagner troops to prepare 'for Africa', Mutinous mercenary boss appears in video welcoming fighters in Belarus and telling them they will not participate in Ukraine war for now', *Aljazeera*, 19 July 2023, https://www.aljazeera.com/news/2023/7/19/prigozhin-in-video-tells-wagner-troops-to-prepare-for-africa, accessed: 20 July 2023; 'Ministerstvom oborony sovmestno s predstavitelyami CHVK 'Vagner' vyrabotan chetkiy algoritm i poryadok peredachi boyevogo opyta boytsami kompanii', Telegram message of the Ministry of Defence of Belarus, 20 July 2023, https://t.me/modmilby/30020, accessed: 21 July 2023.

44 'Komandiry 'Vagnera' pomogut armii Belorussii nabrat'sya opyta, — Lukashenko', *Rusvesna*, 27 June 2023, https://rusvesna.su/news/1687867394, accessed: 27 June 2023.

45 'V Belorussii podgotovili palatochnyy lager' dlya CHVK 'Vagner'. Chto seychas proiskhodit s kompaniyey', *Antifashist*, 1 July 2023, https://antifashist.com/item/v-belorussii-podgotovili-palatochnyj-lager-dlya-chvk-vagner-chto-sejchas-proishodit-s-kompaniej.html, accessed: 3 July 2023.

46 'Prigozhin in video tells Wagner troops to prepare 'for Africa', Mutinous mercenary boss appears in video welcoming fighters in Belarus and telling them they will not participate in Ukraine war for now', *Aljazeera*, 19 July 2023, https://www.aljazeera.com/news/2023/7/19/prigozhin-in-video-tells-wagner-troops-to-prepare-for-africa, accessed: 20 July 2023.

47 Oleg Soldatov, 'Boyets CHVK 'Vagner' anonsiroval 'ser'yeznyye sobytiya' v Belarusi', *URA News*, 28 June 2023, https://ura.news/news/1052661975?utm_source=smi2, accessed: 3 July 2023.

48 Sarah Cahlan, Meg Kelly, 'Satellite imagery shows what could be Wagner's future camp in Belarus, Hundreds of tents were rapidly built to house thousands at an abandoned military base. Whether its the mercenary group's new home is an open question,' *The Washington Post*, 30 June 2023, https://www.washingtonpost.com/world/2023/06/30/satellite-imagery-shows-what-could-be-wagners-future-camp-belarus/, accessed: 21 July 2023; Frank Gardner, Jake Horton, 'Camp spotted on suspected Wagner site in Belarus, A new high-resolution satellite image obtained by the BBC reveals hundreds of new tent-like structures at the site of a suspected Wagner camp in Belarus', *BBC News*, 30 June 2023, https://www.bbc.com/news/world-europe-66052060, accessed: 21 July 2023; Anna Frants, 'See the military camp in Belarus meant to host Russia's Wagner forces', *Defence News*, https://www.defensenews.com/global/europe/2023/07/07/see-the-military-camp-in-belarus-meant-to-host-russias-wagner-forces/, accessed: 21 July 2023; 'V Belorussii podgotovili palatochnyy lager' dlya CHVK 'Vagner'. Chto seychas proiskhodit s kompaniyey', *Antifashist*, 1 July 2023, https://antifashist.com/item/v-belorussii-podgotovili-palatochnyj-lager-dlya-chvk-vagner-chto-sejchas-proishodit-s-kompaniej.html, accessed: 3 July 2023.

49 'Prigozhin zayavil o vozvrashchenii CHVK 'Vagner' na polya srazheniy v blizhaysheye vremya', *Antifashist*, 3 July 2023, https://antifashist.com/item/prigozhin-zayavil-o-vozvrashhenii-chvk-vagner-na-polya-srazhenij-v-blizhajshee-vremya.html, accessed: 3 July 2023.

50 David Sacks, 'The Truth About Ukraine's Failing Counteroffensive And The Peace That Could Have Been', *The Federalist*, 20 June 2023, https://thefederalist.com/2023/06/20/heres-the-truth-about-ukraines-failing-counteroffensive-and-the-peace-that-could-have-been/, accessed: 20 July 2023; 'Telegraph: Failure of AFU Counter-offensive Will Push Ukraine to Make Territorial Concessions, Telegraph columnist Robert Clark has said that Ukraine will have to make territorial concessions in the event of the final failure of

51. the AFU counter-offensive', *Global Euronews*, 19 July 2023, https://globaleuronews.com/2023/07/19/telegraph-failure-of-afu-counter-offensive-will-push-ukraine-to-make-territorial-concessions/, accessed: 20 July 2023; Vijainder K Thakur, 'Ukraine's Counter-Offensive Fails, Military Mauled; Russia's 'Super Weapon' Dents Kyiv's Plan: Analysis, Ukraine's much-touted counteroffensive appears to be tumbling largely due to the Russian military's excellent military tactics and cutting-edge weapons', *The EurAsian Times,* 28 June 2023, https://www.eurasiantimes.com/ukraines-counter-offensive-fails-military-mauled-russias/, accessed: 20 July 2023.

51. David Sacks, 'The Truth About Ukraine's Failing Counteroffensive And The Peace That Could Have Been', *The Federalist,* 20 June 2023, https://thefederalist.com/2023/06/20/heres-the-truth-about-ukraines-failing-counteroffensive-and-the-peace-that-could-have-been/, accessed: 20 July 2023; 'Telegraph: Failure of AFU Counter-offensive Will Push Ukraine to Make Territorial Concessions, Telegraph columnist Robert Clark has said that Ukraine will have to make territorial concessions in the event of the final failure of the AFU counter-offensive', *Global Euronews*, 19 July 2023, https://globaleuronews.com/2023/07/19/telegraph-failure-of-afu-counter-offensive-will-push-ukraine-to-make-territorial-concessions/, accessed: 20 July 2023; Vijainder K Thakur, 'Ukraine's Counter-Offensive Fails, Military Mauled; Russia's 'Super Weapon' Dents Kyiv's Plan: Analysis, Ukraine's much-touted counteroffensive appears to be tumbling largely due to the Russian military's excellent military tactics and cutting-edge weapons', *The EurAsian Times,* 28 June 2023, https://www.eurasiantimes.com/ukraines-counter-offensive-fails-military-mauled-russias/, accessed: 20 July 2023.

52. Aleksey Belov, 'Ne kazn', tak opala. Pomilovaniye, no ne proshcheniye', *Antifashist*, 8 July 2023, https://antifashist.com/item/ne-kazn-tak-opala-pomilovanie-no-ne-proshhenie.html, accessed: 8 July 2023.

53. 'V Rossii nachalas' blokirovka i zakrytiye SMI Prigozhina, V Rossii nachalas' blokirovka i zakrytiye SMI, prinadlezhashchikh osnovatelyu CHVK 'Vagner' Yevgeniyu Prigozhinu', *Rusvesna*, 30 June 2023, https://rusvesna.su/news/1688134317 accessed: 1 July 2023; 'Yevgeniy Prigozhin zakryl svoi SMI', *Antifashist*, 30 June 2023, https://antifashist.com/item/evgenij-prigozhin-zakryl-svoi-smi.html, accessed: 1 July 2023.

54. 'V seti soobshchayut o prekrashchenii raboty kholdinga 'Konkord' Yevgeniya Prigozhina', *Antifashist*, 1 July 2023, https://antifashist.com/item/v-seti-soobshhayut-o-prekrashhenii-raboty-holdinga-konkord-evgeniya-prigozhina.html, accessed: 5 July 2023.

55. 'Russian state TV shows mutiny leader Prigozhin's 'palace' in move to discredit him – video, Russian state TV channel Rossiya-1 TV released footage on Wednesday night showing an FSB security service raid on the office and villa of Yevgeny Prigozhin, the head of the Wagner mercenary group. The package strongly criticised Prigozhin, calling him a 'traitor' over Wagner's armed rebellion against the Kremlin late in June. The film purported to show a cache of weapons belonging to Prigozhin, several passports featuring his picture but different names, gold cars and bundles of cash in both dollars and roubles. Images of Prigozhin's luxurious villa were also broadcast, including shots of a jacuzzi, a helicopter and a large mansion', *The Guardian*, 6 July 2023, https://www.theguardian.com/world/video/2023/jul/06/russian-state-tv-channel-broadcasts-footage-of-raid-on-wagner-head-prigozhins-estates-video, accessed: 21 July 2023; 'Poyavilis' kadry obyskov v ofise Prigozhina', *Izvestia*, 5 July 2023, https://iz.ru/1539913/2023-07-05/poiavilis-kadry-obyska-v-ofise-prigozhina, accessed: 5 July 2023.

56. 'Kompanii Prigozhina prodolzhili poluchat' kontrakty na pitaniye v shkolakh i bol'nitsakh', *Antifashist*, 13 July 2023, https://antifashist.com/item/kompanii-prigozhina-prodolzhili-poluchat-kontrakty-na-pitanie-v-shkolah-i-bolnicah.html, accessed: 14 July 2023.

57. 'Army, people stayed by Putin's side during armed mutiny attempt — Kremlin, Dmitry Peskov was also asked if the president was aware that Rosgvardia head Viktor Zolotov's sons were also officers serving in this force', *TASS*, 28 June 2023, https://tass.com/politics/1639717, accessed: 1 July 2023; Isaac Chotiner, 'What Prigozhin's Half-Baked 'Coup' Could Mean for Putin's Rule, Although the immediate threat of revolt has been extinguished, the episode may embolden future challengers to Russia's status quo', *The New Yorker*, 27 June 2023, https://www.newyorker.com/news/q-and-a/what-prigozhins-half-baked-coup-could-mean-for-putins-rule accessed: 21 July 2023. 'Uroven' doveriya rossiyan Vladimiru Putinu prevysil 78%, VTSIOM: uroven' doveriya grazhdan Rossii Vladimiru Putinu prevysil 78%', *Izvestia*, 30 June 2023, https://iz.ru/1537503/2023-06-30/uroven-doveriia-rossiian-vladimiru-putinu-prevysil-78, accessed: 1 July 2023; Briar Stewart, 'After aborted mutiny, Russian state media mobilizing to boost Putin's popularity, Poll shows nearly 65 per cent of population gets news primarily from state TV', *CBC News*, 7 July 2023, https://www.cbc.ca/news/world/russia-state-media-1.6898524, accessed: 21 July 2023.

58. 'Army, people stayed by Putin's side during armed mutiny attempt — Kremlin, Dmitry Peskov was also asked if the president was aware that Rosgvardia head Viktor Zolotov's sons were also officers serving in this force', *TASS*, 28 June 2023, https://tass.com/politics/1639717, accessed: 5 July 2023.

59. 'Contrary to what some media say, Russia became stronger after failed mutiny', *South Front*, 5 July 2023, https://southfront.org/contrary-to-what-some-media-say-russia-became-stronger-after-failed-mutiny/, accessed: 5 July 2023.

60. 'Uroven' doveriya rossiyan Vladimiru Putinu prevysil 78%, VTSIOM: uroven' doveriya grazhdan Rossii Vladimiru Putinu prevysil 78%', *Izvestia*, 30 June 2023, https://iz.ru/1537503/2023-06-30/uroven-doveriia-rossiian-vladimiru-putinu-prevysil-78, accessed: 1 July 2023.

61. 'OSCE Parliamentary Assembly recognizes PMC Wagner as terrorist organization, The document 'encourages OSCE participating States to reinforce international norms which clearly recognize the terroristic nature of the Wagner Group and its actions', *TASS*, 4 July 2023, https://tass.com/world/1642599, accessed: 5 July 2023; 'Parlamentarii OBSE priznali CHVK 'Vagner' 'terroristicheskoy organizatsiyey'', *Antifashist*, 5 July 2023, https://antifashist.com/item/parlamentarii-obse-priznali-chvk-vagner-terroristicheskoj-organizaciej.html, accessed: 5 July 2023.

62. Pepe Escobar, A Matryoshka of Psyops, 'And Why General Armageddon Is Not Going Anywhere, The main problem faced by Russia is not the Hegemon and NATO: it's domestic, Pepe Escobar writes', Strategic Culture, 30 June 2023, https://strategic-culture.org/news/2023/06/30/a-matryoshka-of-psyops-and-why-general-armageddon-is-not-going-anywhere/, accessed: 1 July 2023.

63. 'Russia appoints top soldier Gerasimov to oversee Ukraine campaign', *Reuters*, 12 January 2023, https://www.reuters.com/world/europe/russia-appoints-gerasimov-top-commander-ukraine-2023-01-11/, accessed: 14 July 2023.

64. 'Russia's 'General Armageddon' is 'resting,' says top lawmaker, The Kremlin has yet to comment officially on Sergei Surovikin's whereabouts', *Politico*, 13 July 2023, https://www.politico.eu/article/russian-general-sergei-surovikin-wagner-mutiny-is-resting-says-former-defense-minister/, accessed: 14 July 2023.

65. James Glanz, Marco Hernandez, 'How Ukraine Blew Up a Key Russian Bridge, The attack severed a crucial Russian supply line and triggered a month of Russian airstrikes. Experts reconstructed how Ukraine pulled it off', *The New York Times*, 17 November 2022, https://www.nytimes.com/interactive/2022/11/17/world/europe/crimea-bridge-collapse.html, accessed: 14 July 2023. Jill Dougherty, Tim Lister, Amy Woodyatt, 'A blast hit a key bridge linking Crimea to Russia. Here's what we know', *CNN*, 10 October 2022, https://edition.cnn.com/2022/10/08/europe/crimea-bridge-explainer-russia-ukraine-intl/index.html accessed: 14 July 2023.

66. Ilya Tsukanov, 'What is 'Surovikin Defensive Line' Which Ukrainian Forces Can't Crack? Ukraine's president has acknowledged that Kiev's counteroffensive is going 'slower than desired,' claiming it's because of his concern about 'people's lives.' Moscow says otherwise, citing the loss of thousands of Ukrainian troops and hundreds of tanks and armored vehicles for miniscule gains. What's stopping Kiev's offensive? Sputnik explains', *Sputnik Globe,* 22 June 2023, https://sputnikglobe.com/20230622/what-is-surovikin-defensive-line-which-ukrainian-forces-cant-crack-1111393818.html, accessed: 14 July 2023.

67. 'Sergey Surovikin calls on Wagner PMC to resolve problems peacefully, not to aid enemy, Russia's Deputy Commander of Russian joint forces in the special military operation area added that he arrived from the front line under order of the Defense Ministry board', *TASS*, 24 June 2023, https://tass.com/russia/1637469, accessed: 14 July 2023; 'Vas obmanom vtyanuli v prestupnuyu

avantyuru Prigozhina'. Ministerstvo oborony RF obratilos' k boytsam CHVK 'Vagner'', *Antifashist*, 24 June 2023, https://antifashist.com/item/vas-obmanom-vtyanuli-v-prestupnuyu-avantyuru-prigozhina-ministerstvo-oborony-rf-obratilos-k-bojcam-chvk-vagner.html, accessed: 14 July 2023; 'Surovikin obratilsya k boytsam i komandiram CHVK 'Vagner' (VIDEO)', *Rusvesna*, 24 June 2023, https://rusvesna.su/news/1687556943 , accessed: 14 July 2023.

68 'Ukraine war: Wagner-linked senior general Sergei Surovikin 'resting', *BBC*, 13 July 2023, https://www.bbc.com/news/world-europe-66183656 , accessed: 20 July 2023; Factbox: Who is Russia's 'General Armageddon' Surovikin, missing since mutiny?', *Reuters*, 29 June 2023, https://www.reuters.com/world/europe/who-is-russias-general-armageddon-surovikin-missing-since-mutiny-2023-06-29/, accessed: 14 July 2023.

69 Pjotr Sauer, 'Kremlin quiet on fate of Russian general with links to Wagner boss, Sergei Surovikin reportedly questioned by security services after Yevgeny Prigozhin's mutiny', *The Guardian*, 29 June 2023, https://www.theguardian.com/world/2023/jun/29/kremlin-quiet-on-fate-of-russian-general-with-links-to-wagner-boss, accessed: 14 July 2023.

70 Ukraine war: Wagner-linked senior general Sergei Surovikin 'resting', *BBC*, 13 July 2023, https://www.bbc.com/news/world-europe-66183656 , accessed: 20 July 2023.

71 Nicolas Camut, Zoya Sheftalovich, 'Russian general says he was fired after criticizing military leadership, accuses Shoigu of treason, 'We were hit from behind by our highest boss,' says Ivan Popov in a swipe at Russia's defense minister', *Politico,* 13 July 2023, https://www.politico.eu/article/ivan-popov-russia-military-general-sergei-shoigu-treason-ukraine-war/ accessed: 20 July 2023.

72 Maria Katamadze, 'Russian general dismissed after criticizing leadership, A Russian army commander has been fired after accusing military leadership of failing troops fighting in Ukraine. The dispute is yet another sign of cracks in the structure of Russia's army leadership', *Deutsche Welle*, 14 July 2023, https://www.dw.com/en/russian-general-dismissed-after-criticizing-leadership/a-66237138, accessed: 20 July 2023; Pjotr Sauer, Helen Sullivan, 'Russian general says he has been fired for telling truth about Ukraine problems, Ivan Popov appears to criticise head of army and defence minister, saying: 'Our most senior commander hit us in the back', *The Guardian*, 13 July 2023, https://www.theguardian.com/world/2023/jul/13/missing-russian-general-with-links-to-wagner-boss-is-resting-says-official, accessed: 20 July 2023.

73 Isabelle Khurshudyan, 'Ukraine's top general, Valery Zaluzhny, wants shells, planes and patience', *The Washington Post*, 30 June 2023, https://www.washingtonpost.com/world/2023/06/30/valery-zaluzhny-ukraine-general-interview/, accessed: 6 July 2023.

74 Matthew Loh, 'One of Russia's most senior generals in Ukraine said he was fired for questioning the Kremlin's war management, and accused his bosses of backstabbing his men and 'decapitating' the army', *Business Insider*, 13 July 2023, https://www.businessinsider.com/ivan-popov-russian-general-ukraine-fired-feedback-boss-decapitating-kremlin-2023-7, accessed: 20 July 2023.

75 'Polkovnik Golovatyuk ob'yasnil, kak otstraneniye generala Popova povliyayet na khod SVO, ' *Pravda*, 13 July 2023, https://military.pravda.ru/news/1856425-ekspert_raskryl_posledstvija_otstavki_generala_popova_dlja_svo/, accessed: 14 July 2023.

76 'Aleksey Belov, Dostuchat'sya do nebes,' *Antifashist*, 13 July 2023, https://antifashist.com/item/dostuchatsya-do-nebes.html, accessed: 14 July 2023.

77 Ty Roush, 'What Is NATO's Article 5? Military Provision Likely Blocking Ukraine's Membership With The Alliance', *Forbes*, 12 July 2023, https://www.forbes.com/sites/tylerroush/2023/07/12/what-is-natos-article-5-military-provision-likely-blocking-ukraines-membership-with-the-alliance/?sh=155858be6c71, accessed: 6 August 2023.

78 'Uchonyye smodelirovali obmen yadernymi udarami mezhdu SSHA i Rossiyey i yego posledstviya (VIDEO)', *Rusvesna*, 3 July 2023, https://rusvesna.su/news/1688359214, accessed: 3 July 2023; Patrick Wood, 'A part of the NATO treaty could turn Russia's invasion of Ukraine into a wider war', *NPR*, 26 February 2022, https://www.npr.org/2022/02/26/1082964072/russia-ukraine-nato-article-5, accessed: 6 August 2023.

79 Matt Spetalnick, Explainer, 'NATO's Articles 4 and 5: Could Ukraine war trigger its defence obligations?', *Reuters*, 16 November 2022, https://www.reuters.com/world/europe/how-natos-defense-obligations-could-be-triggered-by-ukraine-conflict-2022-11-15/, accessed: 6 August 2023.

80 'Stoltenberg: Ukraine's victory is the starting point to moving forward with NATO membership', *The Kyiv Independent,* 15 May 2023, https://kyivindependent.com/stoltenberg-ukrainian-victory-is-the-nato-accession-talks-after/, accessed: 7 August 2023; 'Stoltenberg: no point discussing how Ukraine can join Nato if it does not prevail in war first, Nato's secretary general has said he expects the alliance to agree a 'multi-year programme' to assist Ukraine in its desire to join the organisation, and that there was no 'meaning in discussing when and how Ukraine can become a member of the alliance' unless it prevails in the war 'as a sovereign independent nation in Europe', *The Guardian*, 15 May 2023, https://www.theguardian.com/world/live/2023/may/15/russia-ukraine-war-latest-g7-reportedly-set-to-tighten-russia-sanctions-france-to-send-kyiv-military-aid-live?filterKeyEvents=false&page=with:block-646208dd8f0822aea831dd26#block-646208dd8f0822aea831dd26, accessed: 7 August 2023; 'Stoltenberg Says Ukraine Joining NATO During War 'Not On The Agenda', *Radio Free Europe*, 24 May 2023, https://www.rferl.org/a/stoltenberg-ukraine-join-nato-war-agenda/32426056.html accessed: 7 August 2023; 'Stoltenberg says NATO will invite Ukraine to join 'when conditions are met', *France24*, 11 July 2023, https://www.france24.com/en/europe/20230711-%F0%9F%94%B4-live-nato-wrestles-with-ukraine-bid-at-summit-on-russia-s-doorstep, accessed: 7 August 2023; Jeremy Herb, 'CNN Exclusive: Biden says war with Russia must end before NATO can consider membership for Ukraine', *CNN*, 9 July 2023, https://edition.cnn.com/2023/07/09/politics/joe-biden-ukraine-nato-russia-cnntv/index.html, accessed: 7 August 2023; Lexie Schapitl 'Ukraine can't join NATO yet. But Biden says Zelenskyy is OK with that', *NPR*, 12 July 2023, https://www.npr.org/2023/07/12/1187291581/biden-vilnius-ukraine-nato, accessed: 7 July 2023; 'Ukraine is not ready for NATO membership, says Joe Biden, President Biden, who will attend a NATO summit in Europe this week, said it was 'premature' to allow Ukraine to join the alliance as the war with Russia continues', *Livemint*, 10 July 2023, https://www.livemint.com/news/world/ukraine-is-not-ready-for-nato-membership-says-joe-biden-11688936774832.html, accessed: 7 August 2023;

81 Study on NATO Enlargement, NATO, 3 September 1995, https://www.nato.int/cps/en/natohq/official_texts_24733.htm, accessed: 7 August 2023.

82 Basic Principles of State Policy of the Russian Federation on Nuclear Deterrence, The Ministry of Foreign Affairs of the Russian Federation, 8 June 2020, https://archive.mid.ru/en/web/guest/foreign_policy/international_safety/disarmament/-/asset_publisher/rp0fiUBmANaH/content/id/4152094, accessed: 6 August 2023; Osnovy gosudarstvennoy politiki Rossiyskoy Federatsii v oblasti yadernogo sderzhivaniya, The Ministry of Foreign Affairs of the Russian Federation, 8 June 2020, https://archive.mid.ru/en/web/guest/foreign_policy/international_safety/disarmament/-/asset_publisher/rp0fiUBmANaH/content/id/4152094?p_p_id=101_INSTANCE_rp0fiUBmANaH&_101_INSTANCE_rp0fiUBmANaH_languageId=ru_RU, accessed: 6 August 2023; Russia's Nuclear Weapons: Doctrine, Forces, and Modernization, Congressional Research Service, 21 April 2022, https://sgp.fas.org/crs/nuke/R45861.pdf accessed: 6 August 2023; Claire Mills: Nuclear weapons at glance: Russia, House of Commons Library, 29 March 2022, https://researchbriefings.files.parliament.uk/documents/CBP-9091/CBP-9091.pdf, accessed: 6 August 2023

83 Lyubov' Stepushova 'Vashington ne budet ostanavlivat' Zelenskogo ot terakta na ZAES, ' *Pravda*, 2 July 2023, https://www.pravda.ru/world/1852995-zaporozhye_npp/, accessed: 3 July 2023; Aleksey Belov, 'Bucha 2.0' na ZAES ne poluchitsya?, ' *Antifashist*, 5 July 2023, https://antifashist.com/item/bucha-20-na-zaes-ne-poluchitsya.html, accessed: 5 July 2023

84 Joshua Askew, 'Ukraine war: Russia planning attack on Zaporizhzhia nuclear plant, claims Zelenskyy, Ukraine's President warned on Thursday Russia is preparing a 'terrorist attack with radiation leakage', *Euronews*, 6 June 2023, https://www.euronews.com/2023/06/22/ukraine-war-russia-planning-attack-on-zaporizhzhia-nuclear-power-plant-claims-zelenskyy, accessed: 20 July 2023; 'Terakt otlozhen? Katastrofy na ZAES ne sluchilos', Nesmotrya na mnogochislennyye preduprezhdeniya ob opasnosti,

kiyevskiy rezhim ne ustroil yadernyy terakt na Zaporozhskoy AES v noch' na 5 iyulya, ' *Rusvesna*, 5 July 2023, https://rusvesna.su/news/1688539435, accessed: 5 July 2023; 'Prezumptsiya yadernoy viny: chem dlya Rossii opasen yadernyy terakt na Ukraine, Voyennyy korrespondent RIAN Aleksandr Kharchenko, odin iz avtorov Telegram-kanala 'Svideteli Bayraktara' pishet o sovershenno nevygodnom Rossii nagnetanii yadernoy isterii na Ukraine, ' *Rusvesna*, 5 July 2023, https://rusvesna.su/news/1688547720, accessed: 5 July 2023.

85 'A Ukrainian attempt to retake Crimea would be bloody and difficult, And Western support can hardly be relied on ', *The Economist*, 27 November 2023, https://www.economist.com/europe/2022/11/27/a-ukrainian-attempt-to-retake-crimea-would-be-bloody-and-difficult, accessed: 6 August 2023; Scott Savitz, William Courtney, 'Why Blockading Rather Than Retaking Crimea Might Be Kyiv's Best Option, ' *Rand*, 10 April 2023, https://www.rand.org/blog/2023/04/why-blockading-rather-than-retaking-crimea-might-be.html, accessed: 6 August 2023; 'It will be impossible for Kiev to regain Crimea, Russia believes, It will be impossible for Ukraine to recoever the Crimean peninsula after the fortification works and preparation of the defense of the territory, the governor Serguei Aksionov said today, ' *Prensa Latina*, 16 March 2023, https://www.plenglish.com/news/2023/03/16/it-will-be-impossible-for-kiev-to-regain-crimea-russia-believes/, accessed: 6 August 2023.

86 'Ukraine's counteroffensive against Russia in maps — latest updates, A visual guide to the war,' *The Financial Times*, 4 August 2023, https://www.ft.com/content/4351d5b0-0888-4b47-9368-6bc4dfbccbf5, accessed: 7 August 2023.

87 Barry R. Posen, 'Ukraine Has a Breakthrough Problem, Military history suggests Ukraine's current campaign is far more daunting than the public understands,' *Foreign Policy*, 3 August 2023, https://foreignpolicy.com/2023/08/03/ukraine-counteroffensive-breakthrough-problem/, accessed: 7 August 2023.

88 Isabelle Khurshudyan, 'Ukraine's top general, Valery Zaluzhny, wants shells, plaines and patience, ' *The Washington Post*, 30 June 2023, https://www.washingtonpost.com/world/2023/06/30/valery-zaluzhny-ukraine-general-interview/, accessed: 6 July 2023.

89 Roger Boyes, 'Look to Korea for an end to war in Ukraine, Prospect of stalemate on the battlefield is prompting thoughts in US of a 1953-style armistice, ' *The Times*, 4 July 2023, https://www.thetimes.co.uk/article/look-to-korea-for-an-end-to-war-in-ukraine-q75t066gf, accessed: 5 July 2023; 'The Times: na Ukraine neobkhodimo realizovat' 'koreyskiy stsenariy', *Antifashist*, 5 July 2023, https://antifashist.com/item/the-times-na-ukraine-neobkhodimo-realizovat-korejskij-scenarij.html, accessed: 5 July 2023.

90 'U Kiyeva net sekretov ot TSRU, — Zelenskiy, U Ukrainy net sekretov ot TSRU, zayavil prezident Ukrainy Vladimir Zelenskiy v interv'yu telekanalu CNN, ' *Rusvesna*, 3 July 2023, https://rusvesna.su/news/1688385898 accessed: 3 July 2023.

91 Melinda Haring, 'Russia has not abandoned its goal of crushing Ukrainian statehood, ' *The Atlantic Council*, https://www.atlanticcouncil.org/blogs/ukrainealert/russia-has-not-abandoned-its-goal-of-crushing-ukrainian-statehood/, accessed: 6 August 2023; 'Putin threatens Ukraine 'statehood' as Moscow sanctions tighten, Russian President Vladimir Putin has threatened the existence of Ukrainian statehood as his army's invasion of the neighbour faces stiff resistance and his economy is increasingly asphyxiated by sanctions, ' *France24*, 6 March 2022, https://www.france24.com/en/live-news/20220306-putin-threatens-ukraine-statehood-as-moscow-sanctions-tighten, accessed: 6 August 2023; 'Kyiv says Russia wants to destroy Ukrainian statehood and nation ', *Reuters*, 16 June 2022, https://www.reuters.com/world/europe/kyiv-says-russia-wants-destroy-ukrainian-statehood-nation-2022-06-16/ accessed: 6 August 2023; 'Ukraine at OSCE: Our Statehood's Destruction Remains the Goal of Russia, Despite the Russian troops' numerical advantage, Nataliia Kostenko said the Armed Forces of Ukraine are holding the line and inflicting heavy losses on the enemy, ' *Kyiv Post*, 4 May 2023, https://kyivpost.com/post/16612, accessed: 6 August 2023; 'Putin threatens Ukraine 'Statehood', Blames Ukrainian leadership for war, slams their resistance to invasion, Evacuation of Mariupol fails, ' *The New Indian Express,* 7 March 2022, https://ibbi.gov.in/uploads/auction_notice_liquidation/bdc4a1c9d1c01ccc2cb17aba60fed5fc.pdf, accessed: 6 August 2023.

92 Stanislav Kuvaldin, Why Russia Keeps Insisting That Poland Is Preparing to Partition Ukraine, In the Kremlin's twisted logic, Ukraine is an artificial construct, and only Russia—as the successor of the country that once granted Ukraine its current borders by seizing land from its neighbors—can now ensure the inviolability of Ukraine's western territories, Carnegie Endowment for International Peace, 7 December 2022, https://carnegieendowment.org/politika/88585, accessed: 6 August 2023; 'Disinfo: Poland wants to occupy parts of Ukraine, EU, ' *EUvsDiSiNFO*, 10 May 2022, https://euvsdisinfo.eu/report/poland-wants-to-occupy-parts-of-ukraine accessed: 6 August 2023; Vanessa Gera, 'Polish-Ukrainian friendship masks a bitter, bloody history, ' *AP News*, 5 April 2023, https://apnews.com/article/poland-ukraine-history-war-bandera-tensions-d6a4743ca945dc3144886d9232ed795d, accessed: 6 August 2023.

93 Jadwiga Rogoża, Ukraine in the face of a demographic catastrophe, Centre for Eastern Studies, 11 July 2023, https://www.osw.waw.pl/en/publikacje/osw-commentary/2023-07-11/ukraine-face-a-demographic-catastrophe, accessed: 6 August 2023.

94 'Medvedev nazval printsipial'nyy dlya Rossii vopros v otnosheniyakh s Zapadom, ' *Rusvesna*, 2 July 2023, https://rusvesna.su/news/1688325423, accessed: 3 July 2023; Aleksey Belov: Dlya mira nuzhny prichiny. Bol'she nikakikh 'minskov'!, ' *Antifashist*, 5 July 2023, https://antifashist.com/item/dlya-mira-nuzhny-prichiny-bolshe-nikakih-minskov.html, accessed: 5 July 2023.

Chapter 4

1 Sereni, 'A Game of Shadows'.
2 'Russian Federation: UN experts alarmed by recruitment of prisoners by 'Wagner Group',' *United Nations Human Rights Office of the High Commissioner*, March 10, 2023, https://www.ohchr.org/en/press-releases/2023/03/russian-federation-un-experts-alarmed-recruitment-prisoners-wagner-group, accessed: 20 March 2023.
3 'Ne bukhay, ne voruy, ne nasiluy: kodeks CHVK 'Vagner' dlya tekh, kto vozvrashchayetsya iz zony SVO,' *JarNovosti*, January 25, 2023, https://yarnovosti.com/news/ne-buhay-ne-voruy-ne-nasiluy-kodeks-chvk-vagnera-dlya-teh-kto-vozvrashchaetsya-iz-zony-svo/, accessed: 20 March 2023.
4 Abbas Dzhuma, Vasilisa Nikolayeva, "Krov'yu zasluzhili pomilovaniye': Kak vcherashniye zaklyuchennyye v CHVK 'Vagner' stanovyatsya geroyami spetsoperatsii,' *KP*, January 25, 2023, https://www.kp.ru/daily/27456/4710966/, accessed: 20 March 2023.
5 Yekaterina Lazareva, 'Putin menyayet otnosheniye gosudarstva i obshchestva k boytsam CHVK, K etomu prezidenta podtolknuli deti,' *Ura News*, 16 February 2023, https://ura.news/articles/1036286251, accessed: 20 March 2023.
6 'Bitva za Bakhmut mezhdu 'Vagnerom' i VSU budet velichayshim povorotom v etoy voyne, — Prigozhin,' *Rusvesna*, 29 March 2023, https://rusvesna.su/news/1680087910, accessed: 29 March 2023.
7 Ibid.
8 Reynolds, 'Putin's Not-So-Secret Mercenaries', pp. 4–5. Gabidullin, pp. 33, 49–51, 55, 57, 71, 78, 182, 189–190, 220–222, 243, 246–247.
9 Oleg Tsarov, 'Ot Sovetskogo Soyuza nam ostalas' tol'ko nasha armiya — Tsarov,' *Rusvesna*, 8 March 2023, https://rusvesna.su/news/16/819848/; 'CHVK 'Vagner' - armiya budushchego dlya Rossii,' *Topwar*, 16 January 2023, https://topwar.ru/208781-chvk-vagner-armija-buduschego-dlja-rossii.html, accessed: 20 March 2023.

Chapter 5

1 Frank Gardner, Robert Greenal and Jaroslav Lukiv, 'Wagner Boss Prigozhin killed in plane crash in Russia', *BBC News*, 23 August 2023.
2 Galeotti, *The Weaponisation of Everything*, pp. 55–56.
3 Pascal Le Pautremat, 'From Moscow to Beijing, contractors are the new geopolitical players, 2/3,' *Military Review* no. 55, September 11, 2019, https://www.penseemilitaire.fr/en/_114245_1013077.html, accessed: 9 January 2023.

ABOUT THE AUTHORS

Col. (Ret.) János Besenyő is a professor in Óbuda University (Hungary) and head of the Africa Research Institute. Between 1987 and 2018, he worked as a professional soldier and served in several peace operations in Africa and Afghanistan. He received a PhD in military science from Zrínyi Miklós National Defense University and a habilitated doctorate at Eötvös Lóránd University. In 2014, he established the Scientific Research Center of the Hungarian Defence Forces General Staff and was its first leader from 2014 to 2018. His most recent publication is Darfur Peacekeepers: The African Union Peacekeeping Mission in Darfur (AMIS) from the Perspective of a Hungarian Military Advisor.

András István Türke is director of the Europa Varietas Institute (Switzerland) and senior research fellow of the Africa Research Institute (Óbuda University, Hungary). Between 2006-2011 he worked as visiting fellow at the European Union Institute for Security Studies (EUISS) as well as at the Assembly of the Western European Union - Defence Committee (AWEU). Between 2013-2018 he was lecturer at the University of Szeged, at the Pannon University in Veszprém and at the National University of Public Service (Hungary). Dr. Türke holds a PhD degree in History of International Relations from the Sorbonne University (Paris III EEC-ED385) and received a habilitated doctorate at University of Szeged. His most recent publication is the contemporary history of the Democratic Republic of Congo, Rwanda and Burundi (chapters in a book on French-speaking Africa).

Lt.Col. (Ret.) Endre Szénási is a retired Field Artillery officer and a former strategic analyst of the Hungarian Ministry of Defence. He served as a professional soldier between 1988 and 2023. Following graduation at Kossuth Lajos Military High School (Hungary, 1989), Field Artillery Officers' Advanced Course in the United States of America, Field Artillery Officers' Staff Course (Hungary) he got his Masters' Degree at the Miklós Zrínyi National Defence University (Hungary) receiving a Security- and Defence Policy Expert's diploma in 2022. Between 1989 and 1995 he served at several Field Artillery units in Hungary as a subunit commander. He served as a professional duty officer in Cyprus at the UNFICYP HQ between 1995-1997. He was a senior strategic analyst of the Defence Policy Department of the Hungarian Ministry of Defence between 1997-2023, with multiple fields of expertise stretching from post-soviet policies to global migration, energy security and climate change etc. He retired after 35 years of service as a professional soldier.